Renewing Family Life

Renewing Family Life

In Search of a Silver Lining

Abraham and Dorothy Schmitt

HERALD PRESS
Scottdale, Pennsylvania
Kitchener, Ontario
1985

Library of Congress Cataloging in Publication Data

Schmitt, Abraham.
    Renewing family life.

    1. Family—Religious life.   I. Schmitt, Dorothy,
1928-   II. title.
BV4526.2.S36   1985   248.4   84-22504
ISBN 0-8361-3384-6 (pbk.)

RENEWING FAMILY LIFE
Copyright © 1985 by Herald Press, Scottdale, Pa. 15683
    Published simultaneously in Canada by Herald Press,
    Kitchener, Ont. N2G 4M5. All rights reserved.
Library of Congress Catalog Card Number: 84-22504
International Standard Book Number: 0-8361-3384-6
Printed in the United States of America
Design by Ann Graber

90 89 88 87 86 85 84 10 9 8 7 6 5 4 3 2 1

Dedication

We dedicate this book to our four children—Mary Lou, Ruth Ann, David, and Lois—and their present or future mates. They participated with us in an adventure of family life and a renewal process. At times we have been forced to evolve faster than we desired because they set the pace. Their zeal to explore may surpass our need to slow down and rest. At times we endeavor to raise their sights to the possibilities which they may not see from their vantage point. The outcome is a futuristic family, full of life, excitement, enthusiasm, and optimism; but not without distress, pain, and need for renewal.

Our hope is that they may touch many other lives as they promote emotional and spiritual renewal in their time and place and throughout future generations.

Contents

Foreword by John Rogers 9
Authors' Preface 13

1. Our Experience of Renewal. 17

2. Renewal Is Necessary. 25

3. Romance: A Precarious Beginning 32

4. Creative Courtship. 40

5. The Fragile Family 46

6. Parenting Young Children 56

7. Adolescence: The Family on Trial 71

8. Celebrating the Family 79

9. The Family at Mid-Life. 86

10. Rebirth of a Marriage. 97

11. When the Nest Empties. 108

12. Creative Closure. 116

13. The Challenge 126

The Authors 133

Foreword

In the midst of daily routine, it is easy to overlook the reality of change. We live on a constantly rotating globe that is revolving around the sun, from which it continually receives energy. One finds the same dynamism when one moves from the cosmic to the microcosmic. When change stops within a human or nonhuman organism, the result is decline and death. The issue, then, for the family is how to make the inevitable positive, how to make change a creative process for all who are touched by it.

Part of the dilemma is balancing the inevitability of change with the need for some level of stability. As Abe and Dorothy point out, it is possible to put too much emphasis on either side, which results in damage rather than positive growth. The task then becomes knowing when to be firm and when and how much to relax. It is recovering this balance throughout the life cycle that makes renewal possible. The security of consistency plus the newness of change calls forth the discovery of new possibilities in individuals and relationships.

One of the keys for working at this balance is recognizing

the divine origins of change. It is a gift. It is a mystery. It is God's way of allowing us to live in optimal relationship with ourselves, others, and God. If we could not change, there would be no basis for fellowship, for little good could result except preservation of one's status quo. But we can change; and relationship—community, commitment, love—is important. It is in and through relationship that we grow. It is through community, commitment, love, that the image of God is actualized in us.

Thus the decision to be family is the choice to interweave the processes of change occurring within two persons and any children that may become part of that union. It is embracing the God-given mystery of the possibility of growth into oneness with self, spouse, children, neighbor, and God. It is struggling to overcome self-centeredness to become more truly loving.

It is important to recognize that change is mysterious. In spite of all attempts to learn from previous generations and to pass on our wisdom to succeeding generations, each generation must travel through life for itself. Even when one generation accepts the wisdom of a preceding one, that generation's experience is still uniquely its own. There is some security in following the path that others have trod; but unless one's nurture leads one to totally replicate the life of another, there will be variations that make each journey unique.

This mysteriousness applies to all members of the family though the effects will vary, as will the consciousness of what is happening, what the struggles are. Renewal comes, not through one generation providing "all the answers," but through the continual embracing of each other so that persons can go through the struggles and appropriate truth to their unique experiences—and perhaps even bring new nuances of truth to the rest of the family.

This does not mean that one generation does not share its experiences and insights with another. It does mean that one does not *impose* solutions on the other. Parker Palmer, in his book *To Know as We Are Known: A Spirituality of Education* (Harper and Row, 1983), provides an important perspective regarding this when he says that one characteristic of the learning space is hospitality. He defines this as "receiving each other, our struggles, our newborn ideas with openness and care . . . creating an [atmosphere] in which the community of troth [trust, faith, accountability, transformation] can form, the pain of truth's transformations be borne." It is hospitality that maintains the physical and emotional space that is necessary for persons to face, to embrace, the mystery of change.

Abe and Dorothy provide helpful insights on how to embrace this gift of God that we know as change. They help us to see that rather than actively resisting change or passively sitting by "till the storms blow over," we can be partners with God in the change process within the family. We can be responsible for renewing family life.

—John Rogers
Scottdale, Pennsylvania

Authors' Preface

When we shared the idea for this book with a friend who is a family therapist, he responded, "Most books on the family look at the transitional stages only as potential catastrophies, but you look at them as opportunities for growth and transformation. That's what makes your approach so different."

In many instances the critical phases of family life do result in disorganization and disintegration, but this does not have to be so. The exact opposite can occur—they can be times of renewal.

We are viewing family life as Christian clinicians. We believe that the person of Christ and the Word of God are central to family living. At every critical phase, the power of Christ, the Holy Spirit, can make the difference between a victorious or a catastrophic outcome. This understanding may not be stated in every chapter, but it undergirds the entire book.

Most people do not think clinically. They view behavior as it appears on the surface. Clinicians look for causes that are not so obvious. Who people are, what they think, and how they behave are the result of many influences. Not all behavior is the result of conscious choice.

As we observe the family clinically, we will attempt to consider the factors that play a part in the composition of the family. It is important to note that any current family that is struggling does not stand alone. It has been profoundly influenced by the families that preceded, even to the second and third generations.

The nature of the developmental pattern of each parent from infancy needs to be understood. How the couple established their initial relationship is another factor to note.

After the wedding a new family was formed. Again, a unique pattern emerged that affected both their capacity to relate and their definition of roles. The skills both of them bring influence their ability to transform events into health or harm. There are also many external social factors that impinge on family life. These might be elaborated, but here it is sufficient to show that this type of observation is the essence of clinical thinking.

We are not attempting to study the family sociologically. That would require data from much broader research. Rather, we have chosen to use our personal and clinical experience as the primary source.

The overall objective of the book is to call attention to the crucial events of family life, help the reader understand them, and then show how a family may respond redemptively to all acute crises so that renewal may result. We will also suggest strategies that may be used to make possible a transformation to greater wholeness in family life.

A cloud may hang heavy over our families at this time. We encourage you to look for your silver lining.

—Abraham and Dorothy Schmitt
Souderton, Pennsylvania

Renewing
Family Life

1

Our Experience of Renewal

It was at a special dress-up sit-down dinner at college on a Friday night in the fall of 1952. Long lines had formed in a hallway as we slowly funneled our way into the dining hall. Suddenly, I noticed a new person who was distinctly older than the other students. Since I was a twenty-five-year-old seminary student, the usual incoming student was of little interest to me. This person needed more careful observation. I cautiously tried to assess her without being noticed; but I must have been a bit too intrigued. She caught me looking and smiled at my mesmerized gaze. Her conservative dress and mannerisms appealed to me.

For a number of weeks I noticed her studying diligently in the library. This too was appealing. Then one day I just happened to take a seat next to her and noticed that she was trying to unravel John Milton's dispensationalism in *Paradise Lost*. I offered to help and found a diligent listener to my endless verbalizing. What a perfect match! I needed to talk, and she was willing to listen.

This event involved more than physical or emotional attraction or the first sense of a deep complementarity in our

natures. It was God, the original matchmaker, who had prepared us for this encounter; and he was present in this event.

Our courtship was critical since both of us had come from
previous courtships where we had been hurt. Although
Dorothy's was rather brief, it appeared to have promise until
he ended it suddenly without explanation. Mine was more
devastating.

During the preceding year I had been engaged to a
Saskatchewan girl whose background was similar to mine.
Suddenly, she got carried away as her family joined a Christian sect. Since she felt she had found the light, she assumed
that I would too. I saw only a profoundly changed personality and a warped religion, so I ended the relationship.

Dorothy and I met during our mid-twenties. We had
been bruised, and we both had scarred self-images. Therefore we were skeptical about beginning again. We both
played down romantic love and chose instead to spend endless hours dialoguing about precise issues that needed
unpacking. This certainly diminished the glamor. Little did
we know then that the ability to dialogue heart-to-heart that
we acquired would never be lost. This attribute may have
been a stronger pull toward marriage than all the issues we
resolved en route.

Courtship was traumatic for both of us. Our Christian
faith was a deep mutual bond that sustained us. Although
the scene for our meeting was a Christian college, our roots
were 2500 miles apart, and culturally just as different. It
seemed crucial to share with her my peasant origins. I expected that this would end the relationship.

We spent fifty hours on a bus, during which I tried to
prepare her for an enormous culture shock. But the farmyard and house without plumbing and telephone made little
impression on her. In fact, the experience of the visit mat-

tered very little. She had passed the crucial test.

After this I was ready to give up my homeland, Canada, forever. The United States had been too good to me to feel any loss. This choice really meant that during the rest of my life I would seldom see my seven siblings, my parents, or my many relatives.

The absence of a close extended family, Dorothy's suburban lifestyle, and the conservative, orderly, church service of her background—all felt very cold to me. In eastern Pennsylvania everyone seemed preoccupied with themselves, as they had been for several hundred years. The social lives of people were built around the clan. But beneath this great difference in origin, family life, and church and social life, we felt an attraction since these attributes made us complementary. Also, there were key values that we held in common and cherished dearly: the centrality of Christ in our lives, the importance of the church, commitment to fidelity, and education and children as integral parts of family life.

Our commitment to marriage was made rationally after every conceivable stone had been turned and everything underneath was carefully sifted and examined. Each item provided more material for dialogue.

The wedding service was bleak. Not one member of my family was present, and Dorothy's only sibling was on the mission field. Her widowed mother was the only immediate family member present. Our honeymoon consisted of a one-week trip to Niagara Falls, Lake Champlain, and Vermont, at a total cost of one hundred dollars.

In retrospect, our first eleven years of family life seem almost unbelievable. We moved twelve times and had four children. For only two of the eleven years I was not in graduate school. As a result, I graduated five times and received four degrees and three advanced training certificates. For the first years our annual salary was less than $1,000, and the average for that entire period was under $3,000.

How could we survive all this? There is no doubt that it was a miracle. It can also be understood by considering other variables.

One, both Dorothy and I were survivors. We had to be from early childhood or we would never have made it to college. Both of us went to college with minimal moral support from our families, and I had no financial support. We expected life to be tough, so why would family life be different?

Two, this stage of life came later for us than for most couples. These eleven years were from the late twenties to the late thirties in our lives. Therefore we had more reserves to fight the odds.

Three, our mutual commitment to academic advancement was uncanny. It was as if deeply written into each of our beings was a mandate that education was of ultimate value and it should not be questioned. When we met, she was an instructor in a school of nursing and I was totally immersed in seminary. In each of my applications to the next level of education there was a kindred feeling, as if we were both going to school.

For example, I had great doubts whether I dared apply to a doctoral program at the University of Pennsylvania. No matter how much the faculty encouraged me, I felt I could not put my family through that again. However, I did pick up an application form and brought it home. For weeks I said no more about it. Then one day I came home to find that Dorothy had filled in all the data she could and wondered when I would write out the descriptive parts so she could type and mail it.

Four, we both knew how to be poor and that did not bother us. We had never been any other way. We purchased food carefully in limited portions, and we used all leftovers creatively.

There still were painful moments. One day when Dorothy wanted the local paper, it took a very diligent search of our apartment to find a dime. I then went several blocks to the nearest store to get it. In my absentmindedness I picked up the wrong paper. Dorothy was so disappointed that I decided to go back to exchange it. The proprietor rejected this, accusing me of taking a paper home, reading it, then trying to trade it in for another. Very calmly I told him the conditions under which I had bought this paper. He quickly told me to make the switch. I still wonder if he really believed me.

There were times when it seemed that our family structure was so precariously balanced that only one more unexpected catastrophy would topple the whole works. But as we called forth more energy and more commitment, we survived. During this time I also demolished two vehicles. With no one losing control and by carefully counting the insurance money and with breaks in the purchase of the next used car, we pulled through again.

During this time our commitment to the church held firm. We gave what we could, although at times that might have been only two dollars a week. The children were always beside us.

As a whole, people were baffled by our way of living. No one else was involved in an academic struggle like ours. This came home rather forcefully when we applied to rent a house from a fellow Christian. With Dorothy's careful calculations, it had been established that we could afford it and that the owner would get his rent on time. Somewhere in the midst of the negotiations, he turned to me and said, "Abe, isn't it about time that you stop going to school, get a decent job, and support your family? We just don't live like you do in this community."

Twenty years later, I can honestly say that this entire experience did no harm to our children. I even believe it did a lot of good. They all learned how to manage money. They know how to earn it. They are very goal oriented—perhaps too much so. I have no clue that they have any sense of being unwanted, neglected, or short-changed.

As a whole, we look back upon this phase of life as a time when our marriage and our family went through a trial by fire and we survived. There could have been some scars, but they are hard to recall.

We definitely neglected our social lives during this entire time. We never went out for a meal—not with the children nor alone. We did not have close friendships. We seldom visited, and we seldom went anywhere other than to church. We were so totally absorbed in day-to-day survival that we made no attempt to change this, and few persons intervened. The church community paid little attention to us, but then we also hid our plight and definitely did not ask for nor expect help.

As this phase ended we were chronologically ready for a mid-life crisis, but it never came. I was awarded a doctorate in social work and immediately was offered a professorship at my alma mater. That brought an increase in salary, and within a year I was building a new house. A dream from childhood was being realized. This was just prior to the rise in the cost of building material, so it was easily affordable, especially since we paid for very little labor. The key feature of this house was that the office was part of the design, just in case I should need space for private counseling.

The transformation of our family life happened all at once. Simultaneous with the events just mentioned, a number of other things happened. Our oldest two children entered a Christian high school. If they had lacked social relationships prior to this, they certainly caught on quickly. A second telephone line was necessary to keep their calls separate from my professional calls.

Just as suddenly the church became aware of the fact that they now needed and wanted whatever clinical skills I had spent years learning in a secular university. Before much time could pass, Dorothy and I were on a circuit conducting marriage enrichment and many other growth-oriented retreats.

The only way I can explain this transition is that it appeared that the coin of our family life had flipped. Since we took our children with us on the retreat circuit, they soon became pros at checking in and out of motels and church camps and made friends in hours, if not minutes, after we arrived at a new community, a new retreat center, or at an apartment on a seminary campus. A lot of family life occurred in these settings—and in our station wagon between locations.

The most significant event that occurred at this time was the beginning and the overwhelming growth of my private practice in individual and family counseling. Since the office facility was part of the house design, it seemed right that I commit myself to this. After the practice was well established, I discontinued my relationship with the university. Suddenly I faced the problem of how to be a faithful steward rather than how to make ends meet.

Another phase of family life was now emerging. One by one, the children headed for college. It was not surprising that they caught the necessity for this early in life, so there was never a question of whether to go, only where. The nest emptied so naturally that if a syndrome was present, we never noticed.

A second lease on life in our family came with the entry of the computer. It was our son who made that decision for all of us, and everyone is enjoying the rewards. For the youngest two, it influenced their selection of computer-related majors and provided summer jobs when they were almost impossible to obtain. With the assistance of our son, Dorothy computerized the office practice and uses word processing for our writing—a major calling for us.

We are at a very beautiful spot in family life. Dorothy and I are celebrating. It seems that God has been much too good to us.

We are at the right spot, our mid-fifties, to write on renewing family life because we have experienced it over and over again. We are not finished because we expect that more events will change us and our family.

For reflection and discussion

Before going further in this study, take time to summarize your journey as part of a family. One way to do this is to make a list of key events with details like date, place, time. Then over the next several days try to reflect how you felt about each event and note this next to the event. You might include births, deaths, marriages, particular holiday celebrations that stand out, special church-related events, school events. Hold on to this summary for reference as you proceed in this study. If you are studying this as part of a group, your group may want to discuss these summaries.

2

Renewal Is Necessary

There is no permanent peace within the family. There is no time when the last upheaval has passed and thereafter everything will be calm. There are moments of calm on the surface, but there are many movements and shiftings in the subterrain preparing for the next eruption. The reason for this is that all family members are always evolving as individuals and in relation to each other. The entire family unit is evolving. With that much change, peace and tranquillity are not the norms of family life.

The family is the arena where members work out their deepest problems of living. This is the best place to do it. Employed members of the household enter the workplace and struggle with all the forces that push and pull at them. They yearn to go home for refreshment and renewal, for re-creation. Children endure frustrations and victories at school or on the playground; but the real resolution or celebration comes when they explode into the front door to engage those who really are important to them in their experiences. The family is simply expected to absorb all of these shock waves. So how can there be tranquillity?

Some family members are overwhelmed by these bombardments and begin to dream of the day when they can leave to escape the turmoil. What teenager hasn't said, "I can't wait until I can get out of this madhouse"? The dream of tranquillity up ahead somewhere is perfectly appropriate. Blissful fantasies have their place. They make life more tolerable. But there is no peaceful plateau up ahead. A better approach to family life is to view events and transitions as opportunities for the transformation of family life. We will refer to this as the renewal of family life.

The most meaningful growth does not occur by a gradual movement upward. It occurs in quantum leaps forward. This means that there are periods when life is largely dormant and no particular change occurs. However, the pressure for change builds until the need becomes so acute that all obstacles for movement are momentarily shattered and a huge surge forward occurs. This eruption is a quantum leap. Each of these eruptions can be times for renewal of family life.

An earthquake is a good model of this process. The earth's crust is made up of huge plates that rotate slowly. Entire plates move, but the edge where two plates meet remains immobile. The result is that the two edges do not accommodate the movement of the remainder of the masses. As every year passes the tension between the masses and the edges increases. As long as the power of the engaged edges is greater than the accumulated energy, nothing happens overtly. But when the edges can no longer contain the force that has built up, the energy is released and the correction between the masses and their outer edges is made.

Tensions build up in individuals and families until there is an eruption. The eruption then may be the occasion for a sudden massive change—a time for making the corrections that need to be made. Let's look at the family as having many occasions for rapid forward movement.

Tranquillity is not the final goal in family life. Growth and change are more healthy goals. It is more wholesome to strive for family renewal than for peace. Each major transition point in the life cycle of a family offers an opportunity for drastic transformation.

Too many families look at each eruption as the rubble after an earthquake; they only see the destruction. They are unable to take a bird's-eye view and see that it was really necessary in the greater scheme of things. The nature of the whole earth means that floating sheets of the global surface must turn. The nature of family life also means that these stress-relieving events must occur for members to evolve into the persons they are meant to be.

The biggest task is to learn how to take each transition, each new phase of family life, and realize the potential for growth. Too many families and individuals not only fail to utilize these occasions for spiritual and emotional growth; but because of fear or ineptness, they also react in ways that increase the harm that has already been done. Thereby, they miss opportunities for renewal.

A counselor friend cited a family that prided themselves as having a superior lifestyle because there had never been any changes. This family communicated one dominant message to the succeeding generations: all change is dreadful, so let's not do anything different from what was done in the past. Everyone else may do their thing; but that is wrong. Since we abide by the old rules, we are very special. There is a very clear distinction between "them" and "us." We love each other very much. We show this by sticking together. We take care of each other much more than they do.

We will not rock the boat by taking any chances. This dominant family value was very clearly communicated by adhering to an explicit pattern of living. It was better to do everything the way it had always been done than to do it differently.

The small family house remained the center of the family for many generations. At one time the grandparents, parents, and six children lived in it together. Other arrangements could have been made for the grandparents to relieve the overcrowding, but that was not done. If anyone suggested it, the family responded, "But we are a close family; we take care of our own."

The family attended all Sunday morning services in their Midwestern hometown and always sat together on the same bench. It was commonly known that no one took that particular spot. Ushers asked others who sat there unknowingly to vacate the bench.

The children had difficulty attending the country school several miles away. They appeared ill at ease, as if they did not really belong and could not wait for the day to end so they could go home. There was a pattern of excessive absenteeism due to illness. None of the children completed high school.

One of the family traditions was to recount the fact that the grandfather and father had held the same job for a lifetime. This was defined as stability. They were content to earn minimum wages while neighbors and friends advanced themselves through careful planning and job changes.

The outcome of this family that attempted to freeze time and rejected renewal was rather tragic. The grandfather died slowly of a terminal illness. The grandmother, who appeared to be in good health, died suddenly of a heart attack two weeks later. This sudden loss was acutely disruptive to the entire family system. Everyone was bewildered, but they failed to share their loss with anyone.

The oldest daughter, now in her forties, ended up in therapy for acute depression. She had always lived at home and continued to remain there alone. She also had maintained the same employment all of her life. She had never dated and attributed this to her weight problem, which she related to her mother's always encouraging her to eat far more than necessary. She seemed to enjoy the fact that she was overweight, because she was less appealing to men that way.

A younger brother had a quick romantic fling that resulted in an immediate marriage, which was a major concern of the congregation for many years.

The younger sisters were married, but they had insatiable cravings to possess things. It was not sufficient that their husbands were successful; they wanted more and more. They became excessively attached to everything they possessed, including home, furniture, and children. They suspected infidelity if they did not know the whereabouts of their husbands at all times.

This family illustrates that family life cannot be stopped in time. It must evolve. Any family that attempts to shut down the change process pays a penalty. Each generation that attempts to do this cripples its offspring more and more, and they become less able to adapt to our ever-changing world and their own changing roles in it.

The very opposite view needs to prevail. Change is inevitable, and a family must be open to it. This does not mean that a family accepts every fad that floats by. But it does need to accurately assess what inevitable changes are occurring and find ways to utilize them for greater growth.

In the book *Man's Search for Meaning,* Viktor Frankl

tells the story of his discovery of the real meaning of existence while awaiting death in a Nazi concentration camp. It was in the most horrible of circumstances that he discovered the most beautiful aspect of human existence. Once he discovered it, he was a new person. The more horrible life became and the more certain the end, the higher he climbed. After his release he proclaimed the potential for human transformation in the midst of the worst human predicaments. The outcome of a calamity is—at least partly—a matter of personal choice.

Crystal shared her entire life story in a small group. She had come by way of a very rocky path and had endured repeated betrayals of great magnitude. The lack was in the family of her childhood. Nevertheless, she radiated depth of character, sensitivity, and beauty of personality. The two aspects—her history and her character—seemed in total contradiction until a wise older person caught the true message of her life. "Your name, Crystal, reminds me of a crystal glass factory I visited. At first I was dazzled by the fine glassware in the showroom. It was not until I saw the manufacturing process that I understood. It was really the enormous heat that was necessary to produce such beautiful products. As your name implies, we have all seen the impressive· Crystal; but this is true because you too have withstood a lot of heat. If it were not for the hurts and your learning to rise above them, you would not be who you are today. Visit a glass factory and meditate on the melting process first, then visit the showroom. It will tell you who you are and how you became that person."

It may be discouraging to think that family life is not peaceful, but perhaps peace is not the most desirable goal.

There must be room for growth. And just as individual growth is painful, family growth is also painful and often disruptive. The real art of family living is to use disruptive events for positive transformation, rather than permitting them to become catastrophies.

The key to dealing with each transition is for a family to make an overall commitment to growth. If growth is valued and discussed and the message is clear to every family member, a family will be prepared when a sudden inevitable crisis erupts. That family will be better able to cope, even under pressure; and with God's help, they will survive life's many difficult transitions.

For reflection and discussion

Return to the list you drew up at the end of chapter 1. Note those places where major tensions seemed to come to a head. How did you feel at these points? How did you respond? What were the results?

3

Romance: A Precarious Beginning

Someone has said that a new family begins at the first blush of romance. When one thinks of the entire drama of family life, which may extend for sixty years after this encounter, this seems too precarious. Surely, there could be a more reliable way of beginning family life.

The consequences are so extreme, yet all can be determined in a split second when two sets of eyes meet—"And they fell in love!" From that moment, the destiny of two persons is often determined. The destiny of the children and the children's children are also at stake.

We console ourselves in our belief that God can be part of that moment and of the future consequences. We, as parents, entrust our young adults into God's care, knowing that God is even more concerned about them than we are.

Romance as a way of beginning a family has a lot of validity. It really took a very wise Creator to instill the possibility of a romantic attraction in persons. This capacity reaches across all that separates people from each other and drives them to overcome all handicaps and get close to each other, even to the point of committing themselves to each other for the remainder of their lives. It seems that if any couple knew precisely the entire outcome of such commitment, the reality would be so staggering that they could never make the move. There is some validity to the cliché "ignorance is bliss" in the mate selection process.

There also can be value in beginning a relationship with all of the drama that only romance can generate. This only becomes a problem when either or both parties assume that this heightened state of ecstasy is meant to last forever. It is the memory, not the reality, that should last. Reminiscing about romance can ignite a spark of warm feelings several decades later.

Romance as a preliminary to marriage is precarious. Much of what happens is that the deepest unmet needs of two persons mesh and there is a sensation that in this particular encounter all of their needs will be met and their problems will vanish all at once. It is true that a male-female relationship satisfies many needs, but not all of them, and not as miraculously as it seems at the first blush of romance. So "being in love" also has a very deceptive element. There seems to be the promise that this encounter with another will do wonders for each person, although the true miracle may not be fully realized until several decades later.

It almost seems unfair that at such a crucial stage in life, when young adults are so needy emotionally, they deal with those needs by meeting someone of the other sex and that this then becomes the means to select a mate for life. It is as if persons who are least ready to deal with their tumultuous emotions must deal with them in a way that will affect them deeply and forever.

Romance is a good opportunity for rapid emotional growth. This occurs because such an encounter awakens all of the emotions that have been asleep until now. It also brings them into the open so they can be talked about. It would be helpful in early romance if only talking would occur.

In reality, the opposite is true. From the moment that two young adults meet, it becomes a game. Everything that is said and done in courtship is modified so that marriage will occur in the next inning. An entry from Abe's journal illustrates this.

I am doing a seminar for engaged couples who have consulted their pastors about marriage plans. In all cases the pastors requested them to attend this all-day workshop as a prerequisite for marriage.

As a way of establishing rapport in the room I asked each couple to do a positive, affirming exercise. Each person was to look directly into their partner's eyes and complete the sentence, "I love you in a very special way because...."

The group enjoyed doing this exercise, and it produced a lot of warm feelings and laughter in the room. It was easy to lavish adoration upon each other. I kept on assuring them that this experience was so easy to do now, but that the problem would be that they would find it much harder to do later on in marriage. I told them that some of them would not be able to do it at all five years from now.

I took particular note of one young couple curled up together on a sofa. She chose to do the assignment before he did. She immediately gushed an endless sequence of marvelous attributes at him.

"First of all, I adore you very, very much. Oh, you have such gorgeous blue eyes!" She gently touched his cheek so as to look directly into his eyes. "Such soft skin, and tender skin. You know how to kiss and make a girl feel so precious. I just love you totally as a marvelously, beautiful person."

Then, it was his turn. He slowly turned to her as if to carefully speak the truth. As he halted for a moment, she smiled at him with a deep yearning. The more bewildered he became, the more he sputtered as he tried to talk. Then, she puckered her lips as if to kiss him. Finally, he exclaimed, "I love you totally, more than anything else. You are just completely lovable."

At that moment she buried her face in his shoulder. "Oh, thank you, thank you!" Obviously he had met her full expectation.

Then I chose to do a much more difficult assignment. They were to complete the following sentence. "The one thing that really bugs me about you is. . . ." The purpose was to attempt a conflict resolution exercise and to assess their skill at this.

As the other couples were doing the exercise, this couple was whispering to each other. When it was their turn, she again assumed that she had to go first. Eloquently, and without a tinge of apology, she declared, "Sweetheart, there is not one thing about you that bugs me. We have worked through all of our problems. Our love is so perfect that there is nothing that should bug us." I reminded her that she had said "us." The exercise was for her to speak for herself only. Without a moment's hesitation she said, "I know. It's true for both of us."

It was his turn next. He looked shyly around the room as if searching for words. As he continued to hesitate, the room grew strangely silent. Then she slowly moved her hand to grip his and she squeezed it. He looked into her pleading eyes and quickly echoed, "I believe the same as she does. I have nothing else to say."

Since each exercise was followed by group interaction, someone from across the room challenged him to admit that there surely must be something about her that bugged him. "If nothing else, it must bug you that she does not permit you to think for yourself. Isn't she running your life?"

He denied that statement as she tugged on his arm to pull him closer.

I decided that there was nothing else to do. This setting was surely not the place to deal with that relationship. Inside I grieved, since I already knew that the wedding date had been set. Actually, relationships like this are very common. I simply thanked them and continued with the next couple.

A week later I received a telephone call from the pastor who was to marry this couple. He informed me that they had broken their engagement the night of the workshop. Within a few days the young man abruptly left for a distant location. The girl's family refused to talk to the pastor, and she also declared that she wanted nothing to do with him, ever.

The biggest error that this couple made was that they had romance and courtship all mixed up. This was only the very beginning of a romantic relationship. They assumed that they had gone through this phase and through a marital preparation phase and that the vows were the next step. What was so utterly unbelievable was that there were two families who observed this happening and saw nothing amiss. Romance is only a preparation for courtship, not preparation for a marriage.

It would be helpful for parents of adolescents and young adults to begin to accept that romance is not mate selection. Rather, it is a pre-mate selection stage. The most important function of romance is to help young persons to grow to know themselves, to know the opposite sex, and to learn the meaning of relationship with each other.

This whole event is only preliminary to courtship. The fact that these persons are of marriageable age does not mean that they are emotionally ready for marriage, nor are they ready for courtship. The intensity of the internal emotions have no correlation with their appropriateness for each other. This fact only indicates that both acutely need to be in a love relationship. If that need is met belatedly, the feelings will be extreme. If people could only realize that the intensity of emotions is not an indicator of the degree to which two people are meant for each other, then romance would take on a much saner quality.

If only this young couple had known that it is very healthy to experience the ending of a romance. In fact it would be valuable if each growing youth could experience several breakups—at least one initiated by the other person and one initiated by himself or herself. It is important to learn that the whole world does not fall apart when a romance ends. It only seems that way. There is life after romance. It also helps for a young person to decode the nature of the love experience: how it began, the pitfalls, the beautiful attributes as well as the poor matching, and then be able to compare the next experience with a previous one.

Emotional growth occurs by permitting oneself to get completely engulfed in a romance, be consumed by it, and then be able to walk away from it, heal the bruises, and begin again. Romance should be celebrated for its profound potential for precipitating emotional and spiritual growth.

The most difficult task for parents is to learn not to meddle in a romance, thereby preventing their children from using this phase for healthy growth. The one extreme is to react with such panic that children are unable to experience the growth, or that they experience it in such deceptive ways that they do not learn from it. The other extreme is just as harmful. This is when parents see every romance as the selection of a mate for life and then react as if this experience is already determining who their son-in-law or daughter-in-law will be.

This is a very tumultuous time for most parents. It is especially true if this is their first child. To back off and let romance happen, within appropriate guidelines, is one of the greatest arts in parenting. To engage children in sensitive dialogue is necessary, but it is not appropriate to expect children to reveal the intricate details of a romance.

The romantic phase of their children's lives forces parents to trust that the values that they have instilled in their children in the earlier phases of development will carry them through this phase. This does not mean that behavioral boundaries are not needed. Young persons often value parental boundaries on time, intimacy, and activities. They may test them by protesting, but most often they see boundaries as protection against their own impulses, of which they are equally uncertain.

Romance opens the family unit to an awareness that their family is not an isolated segment in society as it may have seemed until this time. Suddenly some other child from another family enters the home and claims the heart and the allegiance of the young person who until now belonged totally to his or her own family. It may be a rude awakening to the fact that life must go on. The family must be ready to change—to incorporate new persons and to let go of its own—to survive. The romance of a child can be a rebirth experience for all family members.

For reflection and discussion

Think about a romance that you or someone in your family experienced. Take time to describe it in detail in writing (or on a tape recorder). Compare your experience with what the authors shared in this chapter. How did the romance affect you or your family? Was it a growing experience then, or did growth come some time later?

4

Creative Courtship

The interlude between the euphoric high of romance and the wedding date is the period of time which we call courtship. The key difficulty of courtship is to take a relationship that began emotionally and bring it down to being rational. It may seem unmerciful to say that the great emotional high is not the real thing; but it only launched the relationship, which now must come down to earth and face the real issues. Readiness for marriage depends on the degree to which two persons do their courtship homework. The task is to take every possible issue that they can identify and talk about them until there is resolution. Then the couple needs to do one more thing—evaluate how they go about the resolution process.

The more two persons resolve before marriage, the less they need to resolve afterward. It may even be said that whatever two persons discuss and reveal before marriage becomes part of the marriage vows, even though it may not be stated in the ceremony. Whatever two persons know about each other enters into the marriage contract.

A confusing factor in courtship is the relationship between feelings and behavior. Prior to marriage, most couples initially have an enormous amount of good feelings toward each other. They also act very positively toward each other. The behavior originates from the feeling. After marriage this has to be reversed. Two persons have to learn that positive behavior brings positive feelings.

Before marriage, romantic sensation usually overshadows everything. This brings out the very charming gentlemen and the very gracious lady. Then this exemplary behavior results in more good feelings and even better behavior.

After marriage this upward spiral no longer is automatically present. Actually, as soon as two lives intersect as deeply as marriage requires, there is ample opportunity for negative feelings. If a couple is very dependent on the spiral effect of feelings and behavior, the result may be a rapid downward spiral and a sudden clash or crash. Such scenes are common in young marriages and often are extremely confusing.

A couple is not ready for marriage until each has learned that feelings are not the essence of a good relationship; behavior is. And it is within the power of two persons to change behavior because they choose to change it. If either one changes negative behavior to positive behavior, it will result in a change toward more positive feelings.

Another way to consider the desired growth from romance through courtship is to talk about stages of loving. Romance begins with two persons waking up to the feelings of love for someone of the opposite sex. The novelty of that new feeling overshadows everything. It is certainly exciting to discover that the mere existence of another person and whatever special things are said and done between the two create such good feelings. Suddenly all one's priorities are scrambled, and one special relationship takes precedence over everything else. It often appears that it matters less who the other person is than how wonderful that person makes one feel. This may more accurately be called "being in love with love" rather than being in love with a person.

Next comes a shift from being infatuated with a sensation to being infatuated with a person. Now it begins to matter more who the other person is, what that person thinks and believes, and how the person behaves. The problem with this stage is that it is still very self-centered. Much of what goes on between the two is done for the effect it will have on the individual personally. Endearment is expressed, but primarily with the hope of reciprocity. One says, "I love you"; but he or she really hopes to hear the other then say, "I love you too."

The love relationship becomes more mature when the other's well-being takes precedence over one's own well-being. Terms of endearment are now spoken because one believes them and the other needs to hear them, not because one hopes to hear the same in return. At this point, individuals are willing to spend time revealing themselves, instead of concealing themselves, because it is best for them even though it may hurt. When a couple is fully involved in this stage of courtship, they can begin to anticipate a permanent relationship. Marriage, after all, is a selfless venture. It requires putting another person at the center of one's attention, making another feel endeared without the intention of gaining endearment in return.

To use the word *love* for the first two stages of courtship is really a misuse. But since the English language has no other word, and since our society has adopted it as meaning this type of interaction between two persons, we use it anyway. However, it should be reserved for the third level of courtship. Two persons have arrived at the final stage of courtship when they gain pleasure from living sacrificially for the other person rather than being pleasured by personal sensations.

There are couples who skip the courtship phase altogether. They leap from romance to marriage, and only later have the rude awakening that they never worked on the relationship. After marriage they are forced to work on it, but often are just as unwilling and unable to do it as they were prior to marriage.

Every courtship is a family event. Often it is a major event in two families. It can be a period of nagging doubts or extreme rejoicing. Courtship is not a private matter between two teenagers or young adults—or even older adults. It affects the family, the entire kinship, as well as many other persons. The old cliché "you not only marry each other; you marry the entire family" has a lot of validity.

In past years in this country, and presently in many others, it was necessary for the male to formally approach the future father-in-law to ask for his daughter's hand in marriage. Then came the proverbial question, "And, young man, what are your intentions with my daughter?" The expectation was that the young man would outline exactly how he planned to provide for himself, the bride to be, and the future children. Concern for the daughter's future was very much a family affair.

It is unfortunate that this practice has been lost. Parents might use this occasion to ask the young couple to realistically explore their intentions, not just financially, but emotionally, relationally, and spiritually. The health of the courtship affects both the couple and the extended family. So, really, it would be helpful for the family to be involved in the decision-making process.

If your son or daughter is currently involved in a courting process and you could sit down with them for a relationship evaluation, what questions would you ask? Are there areas you could tell them you feel very good about? What areas do you have nagging doubts about? If you measure this couple against your ideal for a healthy courtship, how would you rank them?

Figure 1 provides a summary of this chapter. Feelings are the inner sensations that emerge—or sometimes erupt—in response to another person. Issues are the explicit items that also should be considered in a relationship, such as spirituality, social class, age, education, ambitions, the type of home each came from, and attitudes toward sex, money, children, child rearing, parental relationships. During romance, very little attention is paid to issues because they are

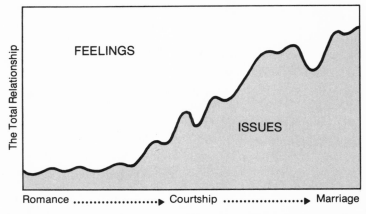

Figure 1. *Feelings and Issues Throughout Romance, Courtship, and Marriage*

overshadowed by feelings. In courtship, the issues emerge and need to be discussed thoroughly. The more this is done, the less sensations will determine the future of the courtship. Increasingly more issues need to be explored even though this lessens the euphoria. In early marriage, issues take precedence and romance becomes secondary. This is the way it ought to be because the intimate details of each spouse's existence affect the other spouse deeply.

The diagram also illustrates the possibility for sudden increases of romance and a temporary forgetting of issues. One hopes that the art of being romantic will not be lost amid the struggles of adjustment. Unfortunately, romantic feelings do not occur as automatically as when the persons first met or touched or kissed; but they may be rekindled.

For reflection and discussion

Think about Figure 1 for a while. Now think about the authors' description of love. Would figure 1 be accurate if you replaced the word *Issues* with the word *Love*?

5

The Fragile Family

A young couple, married only four years, shared a sample day that they randomly selected. The wife described it by talking into a tape recorder as the day progressed.

Both parents are college graduates and from educated families. They met and married in their mid-twenties and are now nearing their thirtieth birthdays. He has a sales position with an international firm that requires much traveling. The unusual fact is that they have a three-year-old and thirteen-month-old twins. This couple displays and expresses a lot of affection for each other.

Due to the nature of the husband's job and the birth of three children so close together, the wife is completely inundated with obligations and can no longer cope. She was the oldest of two children. Throughout her life she always needed and got a lot of space and privacy. Now she has none. This is how she described one February 14, Valentine's Day.

6:40—Wake up. In shower at 7:00. Husband getting

ready to leave for airport. He set the alarm too loud, so it woke everyone. I should have stayed in bed one hour longer; that hour is so precious to me.

Breakfast together. Oldest child spills milk. I do not have a Valentine card for husband. He leaves. I get a hug.

8:00—All the children are not dressed yet. The telephone rings. It is my mother, saying she cannot baby-sit for me tonight. I had tried two other arrangements. This was my last hope, and it too is gone. She gives no reason—simply says, "No, I can't come."

While I am on the phone, I pick up the garbage bag that my husband meant to take out, but didn't. There are a million and one ants under it. The twins are now running around on the ants. I begin to scream. I can't stand it anymore; so I hang up, and I go crazy. Now I am crying hysterically.

And guess who called right after that. It was my husband, from the airport, saying, "I am just calling to remind you to take the trash and the newspapers out, because today is trash collection." I remained civil, took the message, and then lost it completely.

I could not stand it anymore. I put the twins in their separate playpens. The oldest child had already turned the television on and was absorbed in *Sesame Street*.

I tried to get rid of the ants, but couldn't.

I ran screaming into the family room, because I couldn't stand this anymore—the trash, the ants, the kids. I couldn't stand him calling to tell me to get the trash out when he should have done it.

This was all before ten o'clock.

When someone from church called, I collected myself enough to work out some details about a project we are working on.

The telephone rang three more times.

11:00—I had the oldest child dressed and the twins back in bed again.

My oldest child wanted my attention. I gave her some, but I had to try to make several telephone calls to complete baby-sitting arrangements. Then I made lunch for the two of us.

While we were eating, a girl from church came to visit. She brought her baby. She was going to stay so I could go out to do my food shopping. Her child got slightly hurt, so she quickly left instead.

By then the twins were up again, so I fed them. Then I got everyone fed, changed, and dressed. I put everyone in the car. I had my shopping list made out for a change. We all went to the grocery store. Two children were in the cart, and one was on my back in a backpack. It took us about an hour. I got everyone back into the car, and we went home.

Since the kids were dressed, we attempted to go for a walk. It started to rain, so we came home.

I put the oldest child in the bedroom to rest; she won't sleep.

The babies are in bed for naps. I clean up the kitchen and make spaghetti sauce for dinner.

The oldest child comes down to watch TV. I lay down and fall asleep while she watches TV. I hate doing that, but I'm so exhausted I don't know what else to do.

5:00—Babies are up. I get our dinner ready and feed all three children. I bathe all three.

I missed aerobics class. I'm too tired and have no baby-sitter.

I empty three laundry baskets, collect all dirty clothes, and begin laundry.

Husband calls long-distance at 7:30 before he goes out to

dinner. That is the last straw. I cannot talk rationally because I am so tired, angry, and resentful at being left to carry all this alone while he has a late dinner out in another part of the country. He says he loves me and wishes me a happy Valentine's Day. Big deal!

8:00—One of the twins is asleep. The pastor calls about meeting tomorrow night. I get the oldest child to bed. The other twin cries and I get her to bed by 9:30. I clean up house, powder room, kitchen, etcetera. I take Tylenol with codeine and go to bed.

It's raining hard outdoors by now. I have cried off and on all day. How much longer am I to take this?

This woman is not emotionally disturbed nor about to have a breakdown. She functions very well in other roles, but simply cannot handle the requirements of early marriage that have been assigned to her in the process of becoming a wife and mother. At church, where she is very active, she is able to function well as chair of the board of elders. Her pastor often turns to her for advice and assistance. Spiritually, she is a faithful believer and regular participant in activities in the church. However, as she reveals in this recounting of a particular day in her life at home, she is frayed and about to come apart. The stress of early parenthood is taking its toll on her. This account is not unusual. There are many young couples who experience this stress.

An excerpt from Abe's journal illustrates how another couple appears to have found a method of getting in touch with each other.

I paid very little attention to the people in the auditorium as we settled down for a great evening. Handel's *Messiah* is an annual experience of rapture, just as the author seems to have ascended to great heights as he composed it. The huge amphitheater, the anticipating crowd, and the large chorus lining up on stage—all contributed to the regal atmosphere. "This event will again be a milestone at the year's end," I mused. Then the air filled with the tenor voice, "Comfort ye, comfort ye my people . . . ."

It was not until the auditorium reverberated with the bellowing repetition of the combined chorus, "And the glory, the glory of the Lord, shall be revealed, and all flesh shall see it together . . ." that my attention was caught by the couple ahead of us. The tumultuous repetition of the same words continued on and on.

In the midst of this, I noticed that the man put his arm around his young wife and gently touched her shoulder. She decoded the signal instantaneously and slid next to him. Another little squeeze from him assured her that she understood correctly. Very slowly her face turned toward him. At that moment he turned to meet her look. At the exact same time a blissful smile crossed each face. I believe their hearts melted as they each understood the message. Mine did too, even though nothing was meant for me. I was thrilled to watch the beauty of young married persons who have discovered the most delicate meaning of interpersonal relationship that needs no words to convey.

Her body sank even closer to his as she returned to listen to the performance. Her face was like the stillness of the setting sun on a summer's day on the western prairie. This was intimacy in young marriage celebrated in a most profound way.

I now knew that I was permitted to enter into the beauty of the youthful marriage and I needed to record it for myself.

I began to note my observations in my journal. Let's see

now! They look about twenty-eight to thirty years of age. They appear to be parents since there is an air of mature togetherness that is different from early romantic love. Maybe I sense some tiredness. Or is it responsibility, or maybe even suffering that young parenthood so naturally entails? It is obvious that a night out, like tonight, is not a common occurrence. They are celebrating the event too totally for that. Someone must be taking care of their children tonight.

Now the piano begins again as an alto voice and chorus alternately blend together with "O Thou that tellest good tidings to Zion. . . ." At that moment she took his hand and held it gently as they together stare ahead in a mutual trance. It is now that I notice that they really look alike—almost as if they were brother and sister. This phenomenon I have often observed before in married couples whose lives beat to the same tune. It has caused me to frequently speculate that the appearance of a face is more an outer expression of the soul of a person than simply the anatomy. Then, when two people are listening to a common drummer, as in the jointly emerging lives of lovers, they gradually become one, even in appearance.

Often, as the music became especially beautiful, their eyes met and they spoke nonverbally to each other. I believe the message of the moment was, "I am entering into the magnitude of this moment; but I don't want to go alone. I want to make certain you are coming with me." The eyes spoke the message, and back came the reply, "I am with you all the way."

They never spoke a single word, but they spoke more to each other without words than most couples speak to each other with their words.

At one time he did take her program during an interval and point to the name of the next soloist. Her nonverbal response was, "Yes, I know. Thanks for calling my attention to it." How much more was in the signal, I don't know. He may be an acquaintance or a much admired vocalist that they talked about earlier. One slight affirmative nod of the head was all she needed to give to receive a slight smile in return, and the dialogue was complete.

With the downbeat of the conductor's baton, the "Hallelujah Chorus" swelled through the air. As the final performance climaxed the evening, I sensed a climactic moment in this relationship also. His hand slipped around her waist as he commemorated the experience in an intimate hold.

As they clapped heartily at the end, their faces swayed back and forth from the performers to each other. They caught each other's eyes in exact unison and paused momentarily to speak messages of warmth and affirmation to each other. Obviously this was a couple who had discovered the delicate art of warm marital relationship. They also knew the necessity of and had acquired the skill for nurturing it. Then at certain moments, they took time to celebrate that union.

As for me, I participated in two victorious concerts tonight. The one is available annually to anyone at no fee other than to take the time to attend. The other is a very rare performance—the symphony of two hearts playing the music of the soul to the tune of marital love. The latter was the most beautiful because it is indeed very rare. The concert of the *Messiah* tells the story of the historic event when sin was conquered. The newlywed concert tells the victory of two persons who have overcome the gaping distance that separates man from woman. As they learn the art of listening to the heartbeat of their mate, with only one motivation in mind—to love the other—they gradually tune in on each other; and for that moment they become one soul. This is indeed an art that few persons learn.

I do not know anything about this couple, nor how they learned this art at their young age. I would imagine that they tenderly nurtured the commitment they made at the altar, never taking the marriage or each other for granted until they sang the tune of mature love together.

Regardless of what I saw tonight, I am still concerned for them and for the multitude of other young married persons. The relationship in early marriage is extremely delicate and very fragile. Even this couple could destroy it totally. Once the cycle of tenderness that they have developed gets neglected, it may slow down to a halt and a new negative destructive cycle may begin. Then just as surely as this marriage spiraled up, it will spiral down and may be destroyed. Marriages are never made in heaven. They are made of clay and are subject to all the frailties of earthly existence.

The first key to survival in the early years is to accept the fact that there will be a letdown. Marriage simply cannot deliver what romance and courtship promise. Life becomes routine and is made up of mundane chores and events. Just because two persons have found love in each other does not exempt them from these things.

Courtship has a unique way of blurring the truth. It is so easy to make life pleasant most of the time when you can be together selectively and when you have the time to put your best behavior into practice and hide your worst. Then after marriage this can no longer be done.

There needs to be an open acknowledgment that life will be tough. There are so many adjustment factors that have not been, and in many cases cannot be, revealed before marriage. During the first several years after marriage they emerge and must be dealt with. How could the young woman in the first illustration have known that she needed space and freedom and that the arrival of children would affect her so drastically? It would be helpful if a young couple, early in marriage, could tell each other that the "dollhouse image" of homemaking is a myth. Then when it vanished they would at least recognize what happened.

The crucial requirement is commitment to each other and to the marriage. It is the promise that is made in God's sight to remain together forever, regardless of what happens. If two persons absolutely know that, they never need have one iota of fear or distrust that they will ever be betrayed by the other. Then they will be able to cope with everything else.

It is not enough to say that you will remain together because you love each other. Love has so many meanings and can become very complex to define. Thus it is too illusive to rely upon love to maintain a marriage. To pledge absolute faithfulness because of commitment to each other will give strength to withstand the stress test of early family life.

There is an absolute necessity for young married couples to nurture their relationship as diligently as they did in early courtship. If that means a very special night out away from children or other responsibilities, this should be mandatory. Then spend the night celebrating the marriage.

If there are children, other provisions need to be made. Often young couples say that they will not have the night for themselves at the expense of the children. This is not a valid excuse. It is not "at the children's expense" when parents return replenished. Then they can be the parents that they are meant to be.

Effort is the key ingredient that separates those who stay married from those who do not.

There are many young couples who sink deep into a

destructive mire before they have time to build a footing for the family. There may be a sudden clash of values that had not really been examined before marriage. Or it may be that òne or both were simply not ready to give up all their adolescent privileges, and they may revert to them within a few years. This is most often true following the birth of a child, when the young couple must sacrifice so much of themselves for the sake of the infant.

Some couples need professional help at this time. The fortunate part is that help sought at this stage in marriage usually brings quick and lasting results that will change the complexion of the family for many decades.

There are few couples who would not benefit greatly from a marriage enrichment weekend. This is a time to be away from the children and the routine tasks and examine the status of the marriage. It is like erecting a milestone in the marriage, from which a couple may measure the distance that they have come in their relationship, in their role as parents, and well as in their individual lives.

For reflection and discussion

This is the first chapter in which the authors have used the term *commitment* in relation to the male-female relationship. Would figure 1 be accurate if you replaced the word *Issues* with the word *Commitment*? What is the relationship between feelings, commitment, and love?

6

Parenting
Young Children

The decision to have or not have children is very sobering. This is the first generation that can ask the question since the choice not to have children can be made with certainty and finality. Also a major societal change allows couples to choose not to have children without a stigma. So now the decision can be explored honestly.

Giving birth to the first child, and also each subsequent child, drastically alters the marital relationship. It is doubtful whether any couple is not extremely shocked at how great this change really is. To suddenly wake up to the fact that a third person requires more time and attention than they could ever have given to each other is definitely an eye-opener.

The other side is the wonder that is felt as a newborn is held and acknowledged as your own. The child will forever be a product of your marriage. It may be overwhelming, but it is equally exhilarating. All that you may anticipate about the child's arrival is a mere shadow of what it really is like. It is beyond words to describe.

It must be recognized that children do interfere in the communication between a marital pair. The time and attention that must be directed to the children and the exhaustion of child care leave much less for each other. But the other side is that children provide infinite material for the couple to talk about with each other. Since both are so highly motivated to understand their children, they may spend considerable time processing everything they hear from or about them.

Having children also facilitates the maturation of family life. It forces the couple to become more and more selfless and focus their life and energy toward someone other than themselves. This is a necessary experience in maturing.

There is a notion about that says that a marriage ought not to be kept together for the sake of the children. We question the validity of this. Children can keep a marriage together during bleak periods, giving two individuals time to grow and to discover ways of relating to each other so that they can be married because they do fulfill each other's needs. The very process of nurturing children can help parents mature enough so that they can remain married.

A famous scholar on American family life, Dr. Paul Popenoe, also thinks that children hold marriages together and that this is not totally undesirable. "I think that the single largest percentage of divorces involve childless couples. Marriages without children are more likely to break up because there is not much to hold them together, especially after the first sexual chemistry wears thin.

"I have been around a long time [eighty-six years]. I would say that by and large, couples with children are getting the most out of life and are giving the most to life. The nation is kept alive by its children; millions contribute to the happiness of the American home. Of course, they bring problems, but what marriage with or without children, is problem free?"

We agree that children in a family have the potential to transform the lives of two adults, plus the marriage relationship, as parents participate in the transforming phases of their children's development.

Initially, the most common effect of children on a marriage is that parents grow closer. However, in the long run, children tend to drive parents apart. For most couples, the birth of each child is one of the fondest memories of their marriage. An infant evokes the capacity for tenderness in everyone. As we often observe newlyweds in a car, both neatly fit behind the steering wheel. As soon as the first child rides with them, space is made between them for the child. Each subsequent child enlarges the space, until each parent sits at the outer edge of the seat. Even after the children are moved to the backseat, or ride in their own cars, the position behind the steering wheel is never recovered.

This pattern occurs in other areas of the marital relationship. As more and more energy is invested in the children, less and less energy is available for the spouse. Much later, when the children no longer need it, the energy is not reinvested in each other. Take the area of conversation as an example.

Before any child was born, two people could converse without interruption. Even one child may not reduce conversation by just one third; marital conversation may be totally disrupted. Each additional child demands additional time for the right to speak and to be heard. It is not unusual for most family conversation to be controlled by the children.

Then years later, after all the children have gone their separate ways and two people are sitting alone, they may have nothing to say to each other. Long ago they may have lost touch with one another.

The period from birth to twelve years of age is the parents' golden opportunity to influence their child. During this time parents often simply take the child for granted. At times, the child may beg for recognition. If parents are so inclined, they will respond. Or if the child acts out, discipline may quickly put an end to it. It is so easy to allow this phase of development to pass by. Parents are unaware that this phase soon passes. To their surprise and shock, suddenly the child is in the teens and no longer asks for reassurance. Even if parents want to give reassurance, the child does not accept it. What really matters then is that peers give approval.

Parents, please recognize how crucial this early child development phase really is. It is very deceptive in that children are so easy to parent at this time. Don't miss this golden opportunity.

The most important aspect of parenting children during this time is to help them feel good about their emotions. From the day of their birth, children are constantly experimenting with their feelings. However, the value that they place on their feelings depends on the value that others place on them. There is a constant ebb and flow of positive emotions surging through their beings as children experience their world, their brothers and sisters, their parents, and themselves. The validity of each of these experiences depends on the value others place on them. Then they, in turn, also accept that worth for themselves.

Self-esteem is directly related to the value that a child places on his or her emotions. Because negative emotions are so closely tied to positive emotions, when a child has been taught that either positive or negative feelings are wrong, the child will feel wrong about both types of feelings. One error of parenting is placing negative worth on negative emotions and positive worth on positive emotions. It is impossible for the child to sort these. In the end the child will feel bad when any feelings are experienced, and a low self-esteem results.

Many times it is assumed that self-esteem is a direct product of successful accomplishments. This is not entirely correct. One step is missing. If a child achieves in an area that pleases the parents, the usual response is to praise the child. This helps in improving self-esteem because at that moment the child feels good about the affirmation of his emotions. If this is the primary way of affirming a child, it teaches a faulty lesson: that good feeling can be evoked best by performing well. It may cause the child to achieve; but it also creates a fear that if she fails, then warm feelings will be withheld or she may be rejected altogether.

The best method of dealing with young children is for parents to separate feelings from behavior and deal with each in different ways. All feelings, no matter what they are, should be understood, articulated, and accepted. Behavior must be accepted or rejected based on its merit.

It takes love, care, and skill for parents to face destructive behavior. To instantaneously respond to the emotions in an accepting way and yet not accept the behavior is important. In such situations many parents react impulsively and punish the feelings and behavior all in a single action. Here is an illustration.

Your two-year-old is very tired, cranky, and hungry, sitting at the table waiting for food. You are hassled, trying to do your best to get the food ready. As a way of coping, you fill a glass with milk and set it in front of the child. Your irritation shows as you say rather abruptly, "Here, drink this!" The child reacts with tears and anger and dumps the milk. You respond, "Oh, you brat!"

Although the entire scene is understandable from both

sides, it is a very wrong message to send to the child. Not only has the child heard that the action was bad; the child also heard that it was bad to feel tired, hungry, and irritable, to feel bad enough to cry and to be angry.

Let's run this scene by again in a more healthy way. The acceptance of feelings could have been accomplished by simply saying, "I know you are tired and hungry. If you just stop whimpering, I can get food to you faster. I am doing it as fast as I can. Would you like a glass of milk now?"

Another diversionary tactic might be to take one minute, scoop up the child in your arms, hold him tightly as you repeat over and over again, "You are so tired, so hungry, so irritable." Swing the child in a series of circles ending up on a sofa or a soft rug and plop him down, pile pillows around, and quickly return to the kitchen to finish preparing food for him. At that moment you would have affirmed all the child's feelings by your behavior and your words. This also would take the edge off your irritation. Or a moment of humor might permit everyone to recoup his or her equilibrium.

Figure 2 is an attempt to show how feelings operate in Cindy, a child under twelve. The positive feelings are represented by the pluses above the middle line. These are the feelings Cindy experiences when she interacts with people and things around her and is rewarded positively. When experiences are hurtful or rejecting, Cindy experiences the feelings below the line. The arrows to the left indicate another source of negative feelings. When Cindy is in need of positive feelings and these are frustrated, then a positive feeling quickly becomes negative. The arrows to the right indicate that if Cindy owns her negative emotions, many of them become positive.

The delicately cupped hands represent a parent, a sibling, or another significant person who helps Cindy hold her emo-

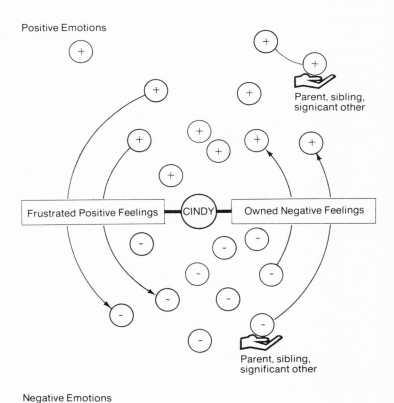

Figure 2. *Positive and Negative Feelings in the Young Child.*
To make a child feel held, it is important to hold his or her feelings.

tions. To make a child feel held, it is important to gently hold the feelings. As children grow older we may no longer be able to hold their bodies, but we can hold their feelings and thereby give them a lot of warmth. To reprimand or to reject their feelings is to leave them with a heavy burden of negative emotions. Frustrations force good feelings down into the negative area. Children are not capable of lifting feelings to the positive area without help. When frustrations force feelings into the negative area and parents do not assist, children begin to lose their self-respect, self-esteem, and self-confidence.

We will return to this diagram again in the chapter on adolescence, when the entire picture changes.

Children need to be heard. Most of the time they cannot say what they need to say; but as adults we must hear them anyway. That takes a special skill in listening.

As a whole, children are known to blurt out whatever they happen to think. This behavior causes a lot of embarrassment to many parents who are very protective of their family's image. This does not rule out that children may not have deeper messages that they need help in expressing. The art of listening to their unspoken messages needs to be practiced.

To really hear the deepest unspoken messages of children requires a persistent and abiding love for them. It means keeping one's inner receiving set turned on and carefully tuned in to their inner world. After many sentences are spoken or a burst of emotion is vented, a message will emerge. You will then know that your child has said something very important that needed to be heard. This type of listening is an art that requires practice.

When our son was only eight years old, a very silent

message began to emerge. At first it was very simply, "I don't like recess at school," or "Dad, write an excuse so I can stay in at recess." At times, it was a lengthy oration on "guys who think they are tough" and "who run the show at school" during all the recess periods.

During these many months he was having more and more difficulty going to sleep, because that only meant that the next school day came that much faster. We asked him to tell us why school was so intolerable. He immediately told us that the boys were playing football these days and he was excluded. When we wondered if only he was excluded, he said, "No, not only me. There are a few others also." We asked him if that meant that he was different. He responded emphatically, "Well, how would you feel if all the fellows got to play football except you?"

My response: "I remember how awful it felt."

"When, Dad?" came the quick retort.

"When I was your age and for ten years after that, until sports didn't matter anymore."

"You mean when you were a kid, they didn't let you play either?"

"Yes, you are right. Even though I attended a small two-room schoolhouse, I was the poorest athlete. And when teams were selected to play against other schools, I never played—not even once."

"But why is that, Dad?"

"Because I also took longer to develop athletically. Since you are my son, you are similar; and you cannot make your body do what it cannot do at this time. I couldn't either."

He was satisfied and returned to school with less reluctance.

His interest in radio and electronics was emerging at this time. As time passed, he began persisting that I had to teach him more and more. I came to the end of my knowledge very quickly. It took very little sensitivity to hear this boy saying, "I have to prove myself in some area that is important to me. If it can't be sports, let me try electronics."

With that clear message, even though he never really said it, we arranged for him to be privately tutored in electronics by a retired expert. The glow with which he returned from these sessions told us clearly that he had convinced himself that he was okay.

The following spring he had to face the same exclusion at school. One day he came home in utter despair. "Today they even chose girls for the team, but not me." In his mind this was the ultimate rejection.

Not long after this, another message came though. He wanted a minibike. This was not a simple request; it was an all-consuming need. He talked minibike around the clock. At every sales outlet, he persuaded us to stop just so he could sit on one for a few minutes and pick up the literature. Night after night he gloated over the literature until he fell asleep.

"Yes, young fellow. We hear you loud and clear. You know you can make your head do wonders for you, but that is not enough. It's what you can do physically at this stage in life that really counts."

The way he fought with the basketball and failed was really pathetic. My vivid memories were too painful to endure this long. So we purchased the minibike. There was no need to learn to ride it. He simply hopped on and rode away. He might not have had the body coordination to play football, but he had the dexterity to make that minibike perform for him without ever hurting himself.

At first, he created a speed course. Four rounds in seventy seconds was his best at first. Then within a week of diligent practice, he smoothed out every curve and used the straightaway for greater and greater acceleration. Now the seconds began to drop. Suddenly the great day arrived when he broke the record—four rounds in fifty-nine seconds. His perseverance continued throughout that summer and the following winter.

He was fighting a far greater battle than just to prove his skill. He was proving to himself that he was physiologically okay, that he was not defective.

The next year he and a group of athletic buddies began building a ramp. They marked the landing area so they could tell at a glance how far they leaped through the air. At first it was only fourteen feet; then finally sixteen feet. With perseverance he outdistanced everyone. The surprising part was that he was always generous with his minibike and coached others to perform their best. He knew he had settled his score, and there was no need to flaunt it. After this he was invited to join the football team and discovered his ability in that too.

Even now, many years later, we often look at that minibike and feel a cozy security within. It is our symbol of having heard accurately the scream of a boy, a nonverbal message that we responded to correctly. By now his sense of self-worth is tested in other ways and success in sports is superfluous.

Responding to and helping children means listening to the unspoken words—the message of their lives that no one has heard. When the therapist finally hears and articulates this to the child and to the parents, parents can learn to listen to that same message and different behavior results.

No family can exist as a reasonable functioning system unless there are distinct and understandable boundaries. There must be recognition and reward for everyone living within the limits, and also some penalty for failure to do so. If the penalty is missing, the reality of the boundaries is invalidated.

Children feel secure when they know they are encircled by limits. The space inside the circle is theirs to use appropriately. The space beyond the limits is forbidden. To know explicitly that this circle exists gives the child a much needed sense of emotional security.

One of the most important aspects of setting limits for children is consistency. A director of a child guidance clinic told us that the most universal characteristic of disturbed children in need of therapy was inconsistency in the pattern of parenting. Emotionally, children cannot tolerate vast fluctuations in what is permitted or what is not permitted from one moment to the next. When there is a constant state of flux, they have nothing they can firmly trust to settle the most crucial questions of who they are, where they fit, or what is right and wrong. In the absence of consistency, their sense of self fails to develop or falls apart.

Where the boundaries are set is the second key issue. If the boundaries are too loose, then the child cannot find them when they need them. If they are too tight, there is too little room to grow. How to find the balance is an art that needs to be discovered in parenting.

At times children's misbehavior is nothing more than trying to find if the boundaries set by parents are strong enough to contain them. They want to know how strong the fences are, so they act up, hoping that the parents will absolutely define the limits and take appropriate action to establish boundaries. Children may even be asking to be punished to help convince themselves that their parents really mean what they have said. Children will then experience the disciplinary action as an expression of caring.

There are differing views about the value or harm in spanking. Children need to know that parents have an ultimate means of discipline in case of emergency. Spanking was that final method for us. There are many parents who use it to vent their frustrations, rather than as an appropriate and considerate method of behavior control. Children intuitively sense the parents' faulty motivation and will be thoroughly disappointed in their parents if it is used in this way. Children should never be abused physically to satisfy a parent's need to be violent or abusive. Be careful in this area!

Some parents argue vehemently against spanking for all the reasons available in the books, when the truth is that they are afraid to do it. Children also read that message. To use it appropriately, as a last resort, can be helpful in child rearing.

Another key factor in setting boundaries is that the boundaries need to be expanded as the child grows, until there is no further need for them. In the end, the boundaries become house rules that everyone lives by out of common courtesy to each other. The child then has become an adult.

One of the most important and difficult aspects of child rearing is the art of helping children take ownership for their lives. The hidden agenda in every aspect of nurturing children is that children assume responsibility for themselves. A child must take possession of her own decisions and be accountable for the outcome of her life. We prefer to use the word *ownership* for this process.

If parents approach a child with the attitude that they know best in everything and then send that message unconditionally, the child gets the impression that her life really belongs to her parents. This may go so far that a child feels that her behavior does not belong to herself at all; so she acts erratically as if to get away with whatever she can because it isn't her life anyway. Here is an illustration.

The father was an army captain before he set up his own accounting firm. He believed in absolute precision, exactness, and accuracy. Since he practiced it so diligently, he quickly rose in rank in the armed services and also succeeded in his business. After all, in both settings this type of precise, disciplined behavior was highly valued. He used this same characteristic with his six children.

The oldest son, now twelve, is as irresponsible as a person that age can be. At school he cannot be persuaded to study. He takes no homework with him and continually lies to his teachers and his parents. When the family sought help, it became obvious that the boy took no ownership for his life. It had always belonged to his father, never to him. From infancy, the father set the exact course for his behavior. The father always felt that any freedom the son took was defiance and breaking boundaries.

The second child, a daughter, behaves exactly opposite— she is completely compliant. She understood the father's absoluteness, accepted it, and used it to her own advantage. For example, she is a pianist who plays music far beyond her age level and even beyond her father's expectation. The task of therapy for this family at this late date is to attempt to help the father give up ownership for every move his son makes and to help the son claim ownership.

One of the most delicate parenting skills is to begin early to teach children to perform for themselves rather than for the parents. This often means that parents do not react with praise or blame when children do something. Rather, parents help children to talk about life in such a way that they can enjoy their own accomplishments and be inspired to overcome their own failures. This is in contrast to expecting children to do well for the parents to see.

For reflection and discussion

There is a lot in this chapter. Read through it again quickly and list the various subjects the authors discuss. Are there any common threads that tie these issues together? Identify them and explain how they relate to the issues. One might be the necessity of careful listening.

7

Adolescence:
The Family on Trial

At no time are most families more on trial than when a child or children reach adolescence. In families with four or more adolescents, it can be a trial by fire. The most disruptive aspect is that adolescents need to express intense emotions.

One psychiatrist has suggested that the degree to which adolescents can venture into extreme emotions is so great that at any one point they can seem psychotic. If adults did what adolescents do, we would diagnose them as sick—but not adolescents. They are capable of experiencing extreme feelings in one direction and with ease can come back from that journey and be ready to venture immediately in another direction. At one moment they are fighting impulses and are ashamed of showing any of them; at the next they can abandon themselves to them completely. They may briefly want to be deeply intimate with their parents; then with one turn of events they can attack them and leave them in utter despair. Teenagers are more idealistic, outgoing, and gracious than they have ever been before. At the same time they can be the exact opposite—selfish, arrogant, vindictive, and destructive.

This capacity to fluctuate between emotional extremes makes it very difficult to discover one's identity. To move from seeing oneself only as an extension of the family to claiming one's individuality is an enormous emotional experience. It is one of the biggest emotional upheavals of a lifetime. But once it is finished, the adolescent can settle down and live with the self that he or she has discovered.

If we use the diagram that appeared in chapter 6, we must change it dramatically to fit the adolescent. All the emotions continue to be present, but they are more intense than ever before. The parental hands are now missing. At unique moments the adolescent still needs parental affirmation, but not to the same degree. If any outside hands are essential, they are the peer group. Teenagers spend enormous amounts of time processing feelings with each other.

It often amazes parents how two teenagers can remain on the telephone for three or four hours. The answer is that they are experiencing each other's feelings mentally and these feelings are generated faster than they are able to verbalize them. Thus, they never run out of conversation material. One person may mention a person, an issue, an idea, or a mannerism and that immediately triggers an emotional response for sharing. The hidden agenda is that they are testing their own emotional responses with each other.

Figure 3 shows that each feeling is tied to the teenager. This means that she now claims each feeling as being herself—"my joy is me"; "my sorrow is me." It no longer remains a feeling by itself, nor is she questioning whether she should own it; now she has to. If she does not, she is rejecting an important part of herself.

The key conflict with parents is over the issue of owning her feelings. Parents are often terrified by the depth of their

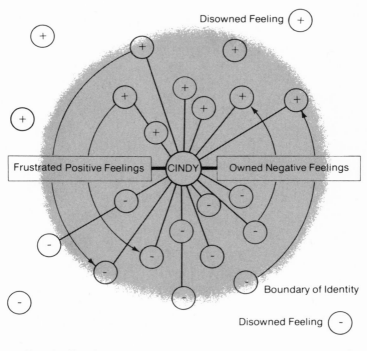

Figure 3. *Positive and Negative Feelings in Adolescent Identity Formation*

children's emotions. Since they cannot tolerate emotions in themselves, they cannot tolerate them in their children. Yet the psychological agenda for teenagers is that either they claim the feeling or lose an important part of themselves. So it is urgent for them to experiment with their feelings. This is precisely what parents find so difficult to understand.

Adolescence ends when all the needed feelings have been experienced and, it is hoped, owned. In the diagram, the shaded area represents the boundary of their identity when feelings are claimed as their own. They have a personality as large as the emotions that they were able to experiment with, experience, identify, and own. The more they claim as their own at this time, the more certain they will be about themselves the remainder of their lives. When children grow up in settings where they are taught to disown, squelch, or hide their feelings, they must then draw a much smaller identity circle. These young persons will go into adulthood feeling inferior, uncertain, and inadequate.

The most misunderstood and often the most traumatic event of family life is the need for and the nature of the adolescent identity journey. Beginning at the onset of the teens, this primarily involves discontinuing their intimate union with the family and then separating themselves until they have discovered their own distinctive personalities apart from the family. Then they begin the journey back again. Due to the difficulty in finding themselves in the current complicated society, most adolescents do not reach the extreme of separation until their early twenties and do not return until about twenty-five.

Children must make the separation journey for their own health, whether the family is ready for it or not. Emotional separation means any decisions that adolescents make to turn from a former dependence on parents to dependence on themselves. It very closely resembles the two-year-old, who has to do bodily what adolescents have to do emotionally. The two-year-old loudly declares that he will put his own socks on to prove to himself that his hands will work for him. After he no longer needs to prove to himself and others that he is capable, he may be very ready to let someone assist him. Adolescents do the same thing, only the task is far more complicated because they have to do it with something as elusive as their emotions.

This is not a smooth venture for adolescents. It involves many surges and retreats. The occasion calls for loud and clear declarations of independence; then—a few hours, weeks, or months later—a rescinding, asking for help.

The surges continue to change in nature as the adolescents grow and venture into the outside world. Eventually they take the final venture. Usually a very obvious sense of stillness and self-certainty surrounds the adolescent at this stage. It is as if a small voice is saying that the struggle to establish an identity is complete. The adolescent now is a person apart from his or her parents—an adult.

Once this struggle is complete, adolescents are free to come home. It is important for parents to know this so that initially bidding them farewell can be easier on all. Only because we, as parents, can trust that they will return can we effectively let them go. This assurance also helps us to maintain the bridges that adolescents will need to make the journey home. The risk is that the methods adolescents choose or the way parents respond can be so destructive that there can be no genuine coming together again.

Many young persons are unable to move in a steady course through adolescence. Sometime during the journey from childhood to adulthood, the inner person is unable to keep up with the outer changes. Suddenly the inner person screams for time. "I cannot keep up any longer; give me time to catch my breath; I'm racing ahead, but I do not know where I'm heading; I have to find myself." Then the young person needs to cop out and let his soul catch up by the passage of time.

Parents usually are bewildered or terrified by this sudden change. A common reaction is to assume that the child has chosen to be defiant. Often this happens to young adults who were especially compliant earlier. This makes the change in behavior so bewildering. At times, it may be viewed as mental illness, which only makes matters worse.

In former generations, this occurred hardly ever because the transition from adolescence to adulthood was much easier. The adult role could be attained more easily since society was simpler. So, as parents, we find it hard to understand because it never happened to us. However, now, we need to understand it to rescue our children.

To understand this as a moratorium—a time for "catching up"—and to tell the child that you believe it is that is helpful for everyone. The child also may be totally bewildered by this driving need to drop out.

The moratorium does end, and the child will pick up again. He will find his place even though he may have lost years and many valuable opportunities. At times, a family may need counseling to assist in navigating the turbulent waters while a child is in a moratorium stage of development.

When parents see their son or daughter create the gap or see the distance to which they must go, they are tempted to move to close the gap. Since pulling them back will not work, some parents follow their children. Suddenly, Dad changes his style of clothing to match his son's. Mom may have her hair restyled to resemble her daughter's. This becomes problematic when parents spend their energy striving to imitate their children. It is most unhealthy when the adults abandon their values because they cannot tolerate the tension that is created by the conflict.

These parents are unaware that adolescents need this tension. They need to venture into territories that their parents have not trod. When parents follow them, it spoils their journey. Worse, the adolescents often need to go farther and farther to find turf that has not been occupied by the previous generation.

The psychological task of parents is to be so secure about their own position that they can stand firm while the adolescents bombard it as they search for their own position. Children need a fixed milestone to move away from. When they need to check out how far they have come, they can stop by home and find an old mile marker there. They may not tell their parents that they appreciate their commitment; they may even make fun of it. But deep down they need it, and they want you to stand firm.

As parents, we must not at anytime abandon our position and assume theirs. Then we only get in the way of their journey. It is our task to keep the home fires burning, so that when they come back it will be warm. This way parents guard the heritage that the young need later on.

One of the most encouraging facts of adolescent development is that they do need to be committed to something. At times, the commitment may be to a car, or to a boy or girl; but it also may be to a cause. Many adolescents make major commitments to Christ. This may be done with such zeal and fidelity that parents are also inspired to recommit themselves.

In dealing with adolescents, it is much better to show them the value of commitment than to tell them what to be committed to. We teach them best if they can see us being committed to our particular values without expecting to pass on what we are committed to.

They want us to live with integrity to our values, even if they do not agree with them. It is better to permit them room to explore what they believe than to impose our beliefs on them. At the same time they really need us to provide a solid footing even if they need to roam.

For reflection and discussion

Compare figures 2 and 3. What are the continuities and discontinuities between the young child and the adolescent? What are the implications for life in the family unit?

8

Celebrating the Family

During a break in the 1984 winter Olympics in Yu-goslavia, a television reporter visited a peasant farm family in a remote mountainous area. The natural response was to view this family in terms of its peasantry and poverty. The entire farmyard was piled deep with snow. They all had to wade through it to do their chores. One could pity the mother making her way through the snow to a brook to dip a pail of water—this was how they got all their water. There were scenes in the barn that were very primitive: the manure needed to be cleaned up; milking was done by hand. A common reaction could have been to wish so much that the simple conveniences of life might be theirs. Our ancestors had it better than this one hundred years ago.

However, with a change of perspective, one could see something totally different. After the day's work was done, all seven members slowly trod toward the house. All used a small broom to brush the snow off their clothing and shoes. As they entered the large kitchen, they showed pure pleasure that the labor of the day was done to their satisfaction. A sense of comradeship pervaded the evening meal.

Though they did not have bowls or plates for each person and ate from the large common pot in the middle of the table, they relished their food.

The most profound scene was two children lying on the floor petting a little lamb. It could not survive in the barn, so it had to be kept in the kitchen. Even the lamb exuded the peace that pervaded all of their lives. The commentator noted that what this family had together in this cozy, though ever so primitive, setting made the drudgery of daily labor worth it. These people were not struggling for a higher standard of living, for more excitement, or for renown. They had exactly what they wanted and they celebrated every wintry night.

We do not need to return to such a pastoral lifestyle, but we do need to recover the heartbeat that gave it meaning. Instead of the events simply happening with the setting of the sun, as they did on the simple Yugoslavian farm, we must choose to revel in family life. Here is an illustration from Abe's journal.

I am now experiencing family life at its best. This happens often for me. Today, I feel compelled to describe it in full. In the past, I knew it needed to be recorded; but the demands of life intervened, the occasion passed, and I could not recover it. Today this shall not happen.

The sensation of beauty is so profound today that I get an exhilaration that permeates my body. This moment demands to be described.

It is Saturday evening. Dorothy and I are sitting by the fire in the living room. Our conversation is low-key as we reminisce about the past. Intermittently we process events that are happening among our acquaintances, events at church, or situations in my caseload. It is probably the peaceful air that the fire created and the contentment that was present between us that gave me the sudden signal that the moment was too good to pass unrecorded. At times like these I am overwhelmed with pure joy.

Life is full of disappointments, drudgery, and anxiety. Then there are periods of simple monotony. It's a shame that we begin to believe that there is no more. Yes, there are also those uniquely profound moments. I now want to explore such an occurrence as it is happening in our family so that I shall not forget it. There are times of pure perfection that cannot be improved. Let me now describe how the events of family life unfolded at this time.

First, I am aware that there is a beautiful stillness in our household tonight. This may also have triggered in me the overwhelming sensation of the beauty of the moment. I do love stillness. I am quickly disoriented by a lot of noise and confusion.

This event is not a fair reflection of our family's experience. We are far too impulsive, outspoken, loud, and at times outright silly. This means that the noise level may reach a crescendo. We have always supported our children's right to be themselves and to express their individuality within limits. Needs do criss-cross and flare-ups do occur. These too are necessary to resolve differences, even if they make us very uncomfortable at times. This also is grist for the mill of family life.

Our youngest daughter is not home tonight. It was too cold for her to walk over to her friend's house, so I drove her. At eleven years of age, they are inseparable. She chattered all the way over, which is her normal behavior. In a very charming way she hopped from the car and called out, "Bye, Dad. Thanks a lot. I'll call you when I want you to get me."

We are not a particularly polite family, but that kind of honest expression goes a long way with me.

This girl adds some charm to our family. She is a born peacemaker. At two or three years of age she could sense family tension and then systematically proceed to neutralize it, even if this meant making the rounds to embrace and kiss every person involved in the dispute until everyone had to laugh at her scheme.

Knowing the genuine gratitude that she will express, one does not mind going out in the cold to get her.

Our second youngest, a son, also is living up to his character tonight. He has a great ability to bring ingenuity, novelty, change, and even chaos. He is too occupied in his project to do that now. He has the capacity to come up with projects at all times. Earlier he presented me with a scale model drawing of the layout for a model railway. At twelve, he is an absolute perfectionist. The design is carefully done. He knows exactly what he wants—a large figure eight to cover most of a four-by-eight-foot sheet of pressboard. He has carefully included his switches so as to have several sidings. He needed help to begin permanently attaching the railway and switches; but as soon as he knew he could handle it, he asked me to leave. He is also concerned that I might do it too hastily and make mistakes. So he would far sooner do it himself. I know he will be blissfully occupied for hours. Give him a challenge to conquer and he is a goner.

After this I checked on the older girls. The fifteen-year-old rarely settles down from her active social life. If it's not a neighborhood group, it's a party or a group event with kids from school. Only one telephone call and she is gone. She has a vanishing act that would put a magician to shame. Tonight she is lost in a novel in the family room. My trip through the room didn't phase her. She is completely absorbed. Sometimes I think, She doesn't read books, she consumes them.

It's in my office that I find our oldest daughter. No one has noticed, but she has been in there for hours on the telephone. I can hear hilarious laughter from outside the door, so I know I will interrupt something very important if I go in. I do it anyway, and she abruptly puts her hand over the receiver and curtly asks, "Can I help you, Dad?" She could just as well have said, "Unless you want something very important, please get lost!" I get the hint, so I leave her. The fact that she is now lying on the floor with her feet on the sofa tells me she has already gone through all the other postures possible for most humans to use when they talk on the phone. When it lasts for endless hours you must resort to this. But all she is really doing is processing normal adolescent life with another like herself.

It is after this event that I returned to the comfortable rocking chair by the fire to talk with my journal. Dorothy is also reading by now.

The one feeling that urges me to write is that this moment just may get lost. And, could it be that something may happen and the tranquillity may not last? There is an urgency about it that demands that it be saved.

Probably I sense that something so ordinary as tonight can really be profound if we stop long enough to celebrate it. Beauty is really in the simplest things if we stop long enough to notice. Then if we do notice, it makes all of life better. Maybe that is what I have to capture tonight.

I wonder if people take time to really celebrate their family experiences. It doesn't take a big event, it only takes a willingness to stop and look. If it's that simple, why are people so miserable so much of the time?

I wonder if I discovered an answer tonight.

Surrounding Philadelphia there are many reminders of travelers of centuries ago. They depended on milestones to locate their whereabouts. The milestones are still by the roadside. The oldest ones are upright fieldstones with a simple engraving—"35 M to P." Imagine a weary family, en route to their farm from an annual trip by horse and wagon, passing the stone and immediately knowing exactly where they were. It told them how far they had come, where they were at the present moment, and how far they had to go.

Modern-day travelers race by these markers, and most probably haven't even noticed them. To many the markers are meaningless.

Family life today is much like the current traveler. People race through life, from one destination to the next, in a continuous whirl of activity until all of life is a blur. There are no clear markers anymore.

It seems that many deliberately fill up their schedules as far in advance as possible so that they will not be caught without anything scheduled. To stop would mean that they would have to ask the awesome question, Why are we doing this? And they would have no answer.

When whole households do this, the house becomes only a central location where everyone returns to prepare for the next event. Since none of the independent schedules mesh, not even for meals, the family members hardly meet.

It may not be possible to change the rat race of family life. However, it should be stopped once in a while to erect a milestone. This means that an occasion needs to be set aside for a special celebration. Or take a time when it just happens that everyone is at the table to reminisce, reflect, converse, and dialogue about the current status of the family. It is important to do this to help all get their bearings. The greater the celebration, the more clearly a milestone is erected.

We simply have to acknowledge that life has lost its significant demarcations. They are no longer built into our lives. So now we must consciously create them. We must do it or else we lose our place in life.

For reflection and discussion

How does the idea of reveling in family life strike you?

What were the big events that were milestones for your family during your childhood?

What are the current rituals in your family? What feelings have you assigned to these? Have some of the rituals become tainted by traumas associated with them? Are there also attributes which give them a beautiful quality?

What kind of celebrations might be introduced that would add value to your family life?

9

The Family at Mid-Life

The period of family life when parents are between thirty-five and forty-five is a difficult one. It is a time when everyone—parents and teenage children—may all be making drastic transformations. What becomes apparent to all is that family life, as they have experienced it, is ready for a major upheaval. Whatever happens next may be drastically different from what was comfortable up to this time. Which member makes the greatest change will be different for every family, but it is unlikely that the family will glide smoothly through this period. Someone, if not everyone, will upset the routine. It will not be family life as usual.

Much has been written on the mid-life crisis recently. As a whole, this sudden awareness that something very dramatic happens to people sometime between thirty-five and fifty has been enlightening. However, it is surprising that this phenomenon was not identified earlier. Surely preceding generations must have paused long enough in the fourth and fifth decades of life and asked these heart-wrenching questions: What is all of this adding up to? Is this all there is? What have I done with my life until now? If I continue, what will be the obvious outcome? What would I want my life to really mean? If that is what I want, what must I do to get there? How soon must I make the change? Is it too late already? Am I reaching the top of the hill in my life, and is the rest downhill? Am I over the hill already?

Then, when they asked these questions, what happened next? Was that alarm button not in humankind all along?

What has been brought to our attention is that most men and women do stop the rat race to some degree and take inventory of life at the midpoint. Exactly what happens after the assets and liabilities are evaluated depends entirely upon the individual.

One of the errors of current literature is to convince us that a mid-life crisis is inevitable and almost necessary to be normal. A popular writer on the subject got so carried away with the theme that the distinct impression was left that all enlightened people go through one enormous upheaval. The theory is that in the course of this event, healthy persons will sort out everything—especially marriage, family, and vocation—and then decide whether it is an asset or a liability. And if it all seems to be a liability, they are encouraged to discard it so that they can go on and attain what life really has to offer.

It is a fact that mid-life crises can be very disruptive—but only to those who have failed to live fully in the first place. Then when mid-life assessment time arrives, they come up with empty hands. However, that is not the way it has to be. You can live your life wholesomely through each of the early decades so that upon reflecting on it you can rejoice with gratitude. Based in your experience, you can anticipate God's continued care throughout the rest of your journey.

This does not deny the fact that at the middle stage of life most people will need to ask those probing questions about the meaning of the first half and the consequences for the second half. But for the Christian, it is a time for prayerful assessment and, perhaps, drastic and creative new ventures. Though secular literature often describes this as a time for unloading, such need not be the case. It can be a time for new joint ventures.

One of the most misunderstood facets of mid-life is that the basic needs of men and women change. Prior to this period, men tend to be primarily outer oriented. This means that men get greater fulfillment, and even their sense of identity, from external achievement. It is the outside world that a man needs to conquer. He feels compelled to get a job, push ahead, climb the corporate ladder, or expand the family farm or business. His image and other persons' images of him are tied up in this pyramid climb. He tends to define his own personhood in terms of how great his worldly conquests have been.

Then when a man reaches forty, or maybe forty-five, most of these things lose their appeal. His deepest needs are no longer outward; they are inward. He may have lost touch with his inner experience long ago, but this begins to emerge as he turns from things to people. Now it becomes important how persons feel. He likely will turn to his wife and children and tune in on them. It can even be said that the aggressive side of him has outlived its usefulness. He now becomes aware of his sensitive side and explores it to its depth.

It has been observed that many men who have been successful in business and have opportunity to move on to higher positions suddenly abandon all and enter training in psychology, nursing, social work, or religion. Actually, second-career ministers are increasing so, that seminaries are establishing separate programs for persons after mid-life.

Vocations that deal with the inner being of persons now have an appeal for men, many of whom shift their attention from the secular to the sacred, or the spiritual.

At approximately the same time, the opposite happens to women. They have lived the first part of life with their inner beings. Homemaking and child rearing are inner-world experiences. For women, the sense of worthwhileness is reflected in the eyes of a newborn child, in the young child beginning nursery school, in the kindergarten child successfully making the switch to first grade, or in the heart-to-heart talk with the bewildered preadolescent child. Another key component of how women feel is the value that their husbands place on their role. It is women in this phase who purchase and read self-help and growth-oriented literature. All of this feeds their inner beings and their spiritual selves.

As the nest empties and calls for her are no longer heard, the other side beckons her to respond. It is as if a woman suddenly hears the beat of a different drummer. She may begin examining the catalogs of the local community college or the help-wanted column in the newspaper. There are many inviting fields for women at this transition point. Some popular ones are library science, real estate, and sales. The computer has made its debut recently, and so it is on schedule for mid-life women who need another world to conquer. It may actually become symbolic of a unique mastery for women, since her worldly-wise mate may be completely computer illiterate or perhaps even terrified of it. So for her to become computer literate is a precise way to establish her unique territory in the outer world.

When a couple knows about this crossover phenomenon, it can be a creative and renewing experience in family life. Suddenly, the excitement of the family shines on mother instead of father. This can be either very refreshing or very threatening. The story of Joe and Janice is illustrative.

Joe received his doctorate years ago while Janice worked. Then their two children were born, and she turned her full attention to them and to homemaking. Although she had a college degree, she did not seem to mind that it had little value to her now. Joe became a corporate consultant, which meant that he traveled frequently and earned a good livelihood. It gave him a genuine feeling of fulfillment to provide adequately for his wife and two children. He was not aware of how weary he had become of his endless job demands until Janice picked up a job as a regional representative for a company that sold eyeglasses. Her job required limited time as she continued her household duties, but she was phenomenally successful. Her business degree proved to be extremely valuable.

It soon became apparent that Janice could earn a larger salary than Joe. What shocked both of them was that there was not a trace of jealousy in him. He actually found himself frequently talking to colleagues about her success. Slowly he got in touch with the exact drama that was occurring in his family. When a promotion that included more territory and more traveling was offered to him, he declined. Instead he asked to be transferred to a different division, which permitted him to remain at the local office so that he could take over primary care of the household and whatever was necessary for the two older teenagers. The most surprising event came when Janice called home from a distant motel to inform him that she would not be home for the night. The reversal of roles was so dramatic that they laughed until they cried.

The outcome of similar scenarios is more often disastrous than renewing. For it to result in renewal, you need to understand this phenomenon in the growth process, accept it as natural, and translate it into a healthy family transformation.

Many men are too unsure of themselves to be able to abdicate their "superior" position for their mate's growth. A man at mid-life who suddenly wakes up to the fact that the house is no longer immaculately clean and a hot dinner is no longer waiting on his arrival home may become disappointed and even depressed. The taken-for-granted housekeeper has taken a job and is zealously climbing upward while he is having that over-the-hill sensation. As she pursues her goals, he becomes more resistant until she may have to defy him to keep going. Then suddenly the future of the marriage becomes a crucial issue.

A most unusual change has occurred for parents who are now in mid-life. They are caught with the need to be loyal, respectful, caring, and in many cases obedient to both their parents and their children. They do not receive a similar response from either. The present adult generation is the first to be caught in this bind.

It has always been assumed that every child would respect the elder generation. As children, this generation of parents learned to give respect faithfully; and as parents they had expected reverence. Now that they are adults they continue this pattern, regardless of how old their parents are.

This same generation gave birth to children who became the "subculture of youth." These were the first children who were given an excessive amount of attention as children. Psychology taught parents to treat the delicate emotions of children with respect and sensitivity. This was all very right, but it resulted in youth and young adults who perceive the world as rotating around themselves and definitely not around their parents. This subculture of youth is the first generation who have benefited from this knowledge, and they will probably pass it on to the next generation.

Although we do not question the value of this change in child rearing, we are concerned about this generation of adults who are left out in the cold. Many adults distinctly feel like they are now caught in the middle of caring for their parents and their children and that no one cares for them. Just as it was their turn to receive, there was a new generation who had not been taught to give.

This change needs to be recognized as a major shift in society rather than the fault of any particular parenting process. One of the causes is that the next generation was the first to find out that they could not learn the essentials for survival from their parents. Simultaneously, parents discovered that they lacked the skill to show their children where they belonged in the future world. Society had suddenly changed so rapidly that the young could not learn many skills from the old. With this, the primary role of parenting became diluted and a shift in obligations between the generations was lost.

Few adults who are caught in this bind comprehend the enormity of this change. They feel only that they have carried out their duty to their parents and have parented as best they knew, but in the end they were abandoned and feel cheated. They may even see their children's failure to recognize them for their life's experience as their fault as parents and feel it must be the result of an error in their child rearing. The truth is that the fault is much bigger than that. The change occurred in Western culture, and they are paying the price for that change.

This awareness often hits this generation in simple events. When it has snowed they do not hesitate to clear their aged parents' walkways. Then they come home to clear their own.

It seems strange that their children who live nearby never come home to help. It might even be worse; they do come home, but only to borrow the snowblower to take care of their own sidewalk. They just might take the snowblower without asking, because they assume that their parents would automatically permit them to have it, just like they permitted them to have everything all of their lives.

The phenomenon was even more absurd in a particular family. Heavy snow fell overnight, so the father, who is a teacher, had the day off. Thinking of the stress this would cause his parents, he quickly went over to clear their walks. His parents were grateful, but there also was a degree of expectation. Then he returned home to do his own. He was just ready to make a fire in the fireplace when the telephone rang. His daughter was calling from work to ask him to clear the snow at her place. She and her husband had to dash to work and didn't have time. Since they knew father had the day off, why couldn't he do it? While shoveling and dreaming of the warm fire, the full impact of the morning's events hit him and he was dumbfounded.

It takes understanding, wisdom, and grace to respond in these situations. At times, single events can be accepted with humor, but a family conference may be necessary to decode and convey the fact that parents also have needs. They do not mind helping out; but there is a built-in danger that they will be abused during a very vulnerable stage of their life.

As a couple enters the middle phase of life, they might make an honest appraisal of the status of their family. The focus would be to consider all the persons involved and the probability of a crisis for any one of them, as well as for the family system.

A risky situation is present when three generations are all

going through a major transition at the same time. An even more crucial one arises when the couple in the middle is expected to forgo their needs for change and maintain a solid, reliable foundation for the entire family, while everyone else takes the freedom for their transformations. Here are some considerations for a family appraisal.

1. Looking at your family in a global way, ask yourself questions like these: Who makes up your extended family? Are there grandparents? Who makes up your immediate family?

2. Begin with yourself as the couple at mid-life. How restless do you feel at this time? First, consider your marriage. Is it in a rut, in a conflict, or is it meeting both of your needs? The most common response of couples at this stage is that several decades of diverting energy to making a living and caring for children have left the marriage unattended. Two people have taken the marriage for granted. Many would, without a doubt, say the spark has left the marriage.

3. If your marriage assessment ranks low, you need to raise a red flag. The marriage could come apart during rough times ahead. Regardless of where you are in the marriage at this major transitional phase of the family, a long heart-to-heart assessment would be helpful with the aim that you recommit yourselves to each other.

4. Is the husband preparing for a conventional mid-life crisis? If this is impending, it needs to be viewed as the most dangerous event in the entire family. The best test is to ascertain exactly how closely you have come to realizing your dreams and expectations in the past two decades.

5. Then, again, the restlessness that is erupting can be purposeful, provided two persons can stay in touch with each other as they prayerfully weigh the options. It may be that you are being called by God to launch out into totally

new ventures that will greatly enhance the meaning of your lives as well as the kingdom of God. To "go for it before it is too late" can mean a total transformation of the entire family.

6. After all these years, what is the wife's position? It may be that she is entirely satisfied with each small step she has taken and is ready to continue for a decade or two. But there may be a restlessness that will not go away and needs to be listened to. The careers of many women are launched at mid-life. The quest for life may have to be settled beyond the family.

Fortunately, the usual restlessness of women at mid-life tends not to be destructive to the family unit. Rather, a whole new dimension of the world is explored. This means that the family should be ready to make sacrifices and encourage her to see who she can be outside the family.

7. Next the grandparents need to be considered. How heavily do they weigh on the family unit? It may be very heavy or not at all. Sometimes the weight can be the expectation that nobody will make any drastic changes because this threatens them and their future. It can be a loud message or a subtle one that says, "That is just not the way it ought to be done."

8. Where are the children at this stage in life? The ideal is that they are finding their own place in the world with determination and effectiveness. Then parents realize that the burden of parenting is rapidly ending and the children are, in fact, setting them free to make the necessary decisions that will enable the second half of their lives to be even more meaningful than the first half.

9. The most critical family drama at mid-life is when every member is going through a major transitional crisis at the same time. Then everyone is so caught up in his or her

turmoil that there is little, if any, mutual support. Grandparents may proceed to close their life's work in a most irrational way. Father may be engulfed in his unfulfilled life and be in the process of throwing it away to find all at once what he has been yearning for. Mother may abandon what she experienced as a depressing homemaking role to explore the world. The children may be in their own adolescent crises, or in a moratorium, unable to find themselves. This is extreme but not that uncommon in today's society.

10. The goal is to come through the middle stage of family life rejuvenated and healthy. It can be done by prayerful, honest, unselfish, and clearheaded navigation.

For reflection and discussion

Review the authors' discussion of what they called "the male-female crossover" at mid-life. How does this fit your experience? Do you think this fits most younger couples today? If not, how would you change figure 4?

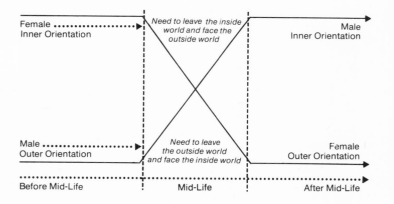

Figure 4.   *Male-Female Crossover at Mid-Life*

10

Rebirth of a Marriage

There was an air of compassionate mystery that encircled this couple. No one in the group could miss it. It was too conspicuous. The way Dave ushered Iva into the room, the way he helped her with her coat and then had her seated in the group—men over forty just don't treat their wives this delicately. Oh, you see it once in a while in a public place, but then it is so dramatic that it is obvious that it is a show. Here it was genuine. There was nothing unnatural about it. The performance was not rehearsed. It had been repeated so many times they were not aware that it was different. She was carried into the room on a gold platter and he was privileged to carry the platter.

Of all places to do it—a marriage renewal weekend. One may expect a high degree of nervousness or awkwardness at the beginning. And be assured that most couples do come with deep unresolved pain that they are desperately trying to hide. The initial politeness or gentleness is almost always so stylized that it seems preprogrammed for the occasion.

The way this couple began in the group only deepened

The story of Iva and Dave is from Abe's journal.

the mystery. Why had they come such a great distance? He touched her gently on the shoulder and said, "I have only begun to love her. I want to go on and on." And her response was equally promising. "Sweetheart, I want to take one more step higher with you." That was why they said they came!

The thought that crossed my mind was, "This couple defies my notion of marriage—twenty years of marriage and five children later and no more than an eighth-grade education. He was unable to write and came from a large farm in the Midwest. They appeared to have arrived at the pinnacle of marriage so naturally. For years I have been saying, 'Show me just one couple who has reached the fairy-tale ideal—and they lived happily ever after—without the valley of despair and purification, then I will reconsider my model for marriage. Is this the couple I'm looking for? Is this couple an exception to the rule?' "

Some clues from their childhood created more uncertainty rather than bringing a solution. Each came from large rural families. Hers was a well-to-do, prosperous farm family, whereas his was a financial disaster. Although each recalled pleasant times in their large family gatherings, each enumerated more agony than fulfillment. From his early teens he was required to work very hard as a farmhand for neighbors. He felt very little self-worth other than that he could provide for the family's survival. She was lost in the crowd all her life—not nearly as good-looking or as popular as her sisters, a loner and a loser.

From my awareness of the effect of childhood development and the role of the family's interaction in preparation for marriage, I saw few positive attributes. Theoretically this couple would have a marginal marriage at best, perhaps a tragedy.

When the task on courtship was shared in the group, very good vibrations were obvious. Dave and Iva very carefully had sorted out each other in a large crowd of youth who socialized together in their rural neighborhood. He was looking for "beauty of the heart, not beauty of the skin," and this he found in Iva. He was ecstatic when she responded to his beckoning. She needed someone to believe in her. For once she needed to be the uncontested "first" in someone's life. He left no doubt in her mind that she was special.

At least this marriage had a fairy-tale beginning. They believed beyond a shadow of a doubt that they were meant for each other. God, in providing for his children, had supervised this meeting and had led them all the way to marriage.

The many tender touches caused a degree of uneasiness in the room. The other couples could not do this. The painful marriages that others brought into the group were already being described. To have such a sharp contrast was disconcerting. Yet no one really confronted the issue. Oh, there was some kidding, such as calling them "lovey-dovey," but that was only in passing.

I even noticed that this couple didn't seem startled when a couple with a stormy marriage announced, "If any one of you can figure out why we got married, you deserve a prize. We think we were incompatible from the day we laid eyes on each other, and we have spent ten years proving that it's true."

Iva and Dave found the task on conflict resolution difficult to handle. They played around with a few minor complaints about each other, but really passed by this part of the group experience. She sputtered out something like, "All he has to do is touch me anywhere and I melt like butter." This brought hearty laughter but no light. Could anyone ques-

tion this description? Hardly, because whatever one cited as
annoying the other simply accepted, giving supporting evidence of how this trait fit his or her personality and childhood development. Then he or she promised to begin a
program of remedial activity. To have brought it out in the
open was all that was necessary to begin the resolution
process.

By now, my internal monitor was screaming, "This is not
the full story!"

On the fourth group task, and well past the midpoint of
the weekend retreat, we all were let in on a revelation. The
task was simply to make some form of personal commitment
to each other so as to facilitate future marital growth. It
wasn't the task that encouraged them to begin letting us
know the other side. It was that the story was so intensely
personal and so excruciatingly painful that they were very
careful to wait for the right occasion. Their own trust level
was one variable. The second was that they did not want to
dump this on the group prematurely. I even think that they
knew that to tell the group this would cause a major shift, so
they responsibly waited. There was no question that they
had full intentions of sharing it.

They began by saying that what we were now seeing in
their marriage had not always been the case. Yes, they were
deeply infatuated with each other at the beginning, and
nothing they had said thus far was an error. Through their
marriage they were always civil and kind to each other.
They agreed on child rearing and on much of the daily
routine of farm life.

Then came the big "But!" First Dave spoke. "As you may
well expect, I was never close to anyone in my childhood.
Sure I was accepted, but only as one of the crowd and primarily based on work output. When our children began ar-

riving, I moved to the fringe of the family. I found it very, very difficult to be close to Iva. With five children around her, it wasn't easy to get near; but then I couldn't even try."

Then Iva picked up the story. "During those years I was simply piled under work—diapers, bottles, and more diapers and bottles. Now, I didn't mind this. I wanted a big family. I had pleasant enough memories of my family that this did not bother me. But what did bother me was that I felt so totally worthless. I had these terribly lonely feelings. I just wanted someone to listen to me—just meet me to the depth that I needed to be met. But the more I reached out toward Dave, the more he eluded me."

"But, you know, I didn't know how," Dave added. "I was even frightened of getting close to anyone—and most of all, you. I simply couldn't stand those tears and more tears. Here I would come in from the farmyard for lunch; and no sooner did I step into the house, than you dissolved into tears."

"And I couldn't understand my tears either, or else I would have told you. I was just empty inside. All I could sense was that I was feeling more and more worthless as the years went by. You didn't know how to reach me. The more I cried, the farther away I drove you. Then you came with those easy answers that made matters only worse. 'Think of the beauty of life. Look at the blue sky, the bountiful fields of wheat. We were once so poor; now look how God has blessed us!' I knew you were right, and that made me feel even worse. Now I was really absolutely no good. I couldn't be grateful. I should be. Every fact you said was true, and I could do nothing about it. I now know I needed you to listen to me, believe in me, assure me, and touch me so that some-one out there would get through to me to still my soul that kept screaming at me, 'I am no good.' I thought I had to ac-cept your simple solutions. The more I was unable to, the lower I went and the more I cried."

Then Dave stepped in as if he had to take responsibility for what now had to be said. As they were talking their hands tenderly touched each other. Many moments were baptized with tears. Wiping away tears was a common experience around the room since the emotions were just too intense to communicate verbally. In a sacred setting like this, it was all right and even fitting. Everyone knew it.

"One Saturday night," Dave began, "only a few years ago, we had some harsh words. I had all I could take, so I stomped off into the bedroom and resolved not to come out until she came to ask forgiveness. I really felt sorry for myself, just as I had all my life. I was pouting like a child. I stayed there for at least an hour. When she didn't come and I heard nothing from her, I went looking for her. She was sound asleep on the sofa. Then I went into the kitchen for a drink of water.

"Then I spotted a note on the table: 'I love you, honey! But I am now going to set you free to be happy. I have taken the whole bottle of sleeping pills. You will be happy with someone else. I am only a burden to you and to the children. Go find yourself the kind of wife you deserve. The children also need a better mother than I am. I am doing this because I love you. Iva.' "

By now he broke down sobbing and could not go on. His wife picked up the thread of the story.

"As he opened the cupboard door, I woke. The first thought that crossed my mind was that he had read the note, thought I was dead, and was taking pills. I leaped to my feet and ran for him and hugged him, and we both stood there gushing with tears. It took a long time before we sat down in the living room to talk. I had taken no pills. I simply fell asleep after writing the note.

"In the midst of his tears, he told me over and over again how much he loved me, how much he needed me, and that I should not and could not go. We talked the rest of the night—for eight hours. We cried over and over again.

"I had never seen him cry before. That felt so good. Now I knew he needed me. He was with me. That was what I needed, not just his simple solutions. What I needed was him, not just an answer to my problem.

"You can't imagine how much we talked that night. And this man who had hardly anything to say couldn't stop talking. It just poured out like a river."

Someone in the group wanted to know if that was the total answer. Iva remarked that it was not. They felt better, but she still had a lot of fear that the depression would return. Several months later they went to a retreat for spiritual renewal. They had a very good experience.

The group concluded that they had hit bottom and that this renewal experience was their first high. True to form, there was a valley experience that followed.

Then one night, months later, alone in their bed, they talked about her persistent fear that the depression would return. She had been reading a book about casting out evil spirits and wondered if this was not what they needed to do. He agreed, so they knelt in prayer and asked God to come and, through the power of the Holy Spirit, remove this evil spirit that had been plaguing her. Nothing happened. Then he rose to his feet, laid his hands on her head and addressed the evil spirit by name, "Nerves—the evil spirit of nerves—in the name of Jesus get out of my wife." She immediately sensed a burden had lifted, "as if a presence departed from within me." She then began laughing and finally began praying and rejoicing. That was when this couple entered an extremely ecstatic phase of their marriage.

They have not remained at that peak, as no one does. They freely told of conflicts they have that are similar to those of other people. At times they may exchange sharp words, as that is a necessary part of marriage. However, there have been no long periods of alienation or depression.

Just prior to coming to this weekend marriage retreat, Iva suddenly began sinking into gloom. No doubt the fear of this type of exposure contributed to it. At that time he said to her, "Honey, have you tried your prayer language?" He kept on encouraging her to continue this experience longer and longer, when suddenly she felt "as if a presence entered the room, picked up the burden and left with it." And they rejoiced again.

At the end, he said, "I was really afraid to come to this weekend. The whole experience for the last several years has been humiliating for me, and you all know I have a problem with pride. It was my pride that kept me from reaching out to her all those years when she was sinking. But that horrible night knocked all my pride to bits, except when I began thinking about coming here and that we would tell this story. I knew it would be humiliating. Because I like to handle my own life, I kept on telling my wife to handle hers; but that is no way to handle marriage. It is surrendering out of total helplessness that is the beginning of marriage. It is through surrender that we won the victory."

I exclaimed, "Oh, man, are you ever profound. You are telling it like I have never heard it before. It's just beautiful! You have made us sob together and rejoice together, and we are all more whole for it."

"Thank you," he said, in the midst of tears. "It's all of the Lord. He wanted us here today.

"Another reason I was afraid to come was that I thought our experience was so mystical that you wouldn't understand it. Or even worse, I thought that you, with all your training in psychology, would decide it was psychotic."

I exploded, "Never in my life! This is not psychosis; this is mental and spiritual health at its best."

Then I quickly turned to the couple who came to this retreat in the midst of a devastated marriage and asked, "In one word, how does this make you feel about your marriage?"

Back came an answer, just as quickly, "Hopeful!"

Then Dave and Iva put the grand finale on the session. "Look, I don't want anyone to think that we have given you a recipe or a road map for your marriage. It's just the journey we had to take. You, all, have yours. I hope this can give you courage to take it."

The group affirmed that this was beautifully said.

As we left this marriage retreat in a state of ecstasy, we began wondering why this couple came. This was not their first attempt to enroll. They had left all their children to fend for themselves far away.

Slowly we recreated an answer. They needed to test this experience with a community of caring persons under professional and psychological leadership. And that was good! This would give them an intellectual and rational hold on the experience. How much they needed this was indicated by the risk they took in having it be labeled "sick," yet they came—but then courage was not foreign to this couple.

Our notion was confirmed five days after the retreat when we received this letter from Iva. On the face of the letter was the inscription: "The heart that loves is always young."

Dear Abe and Dorothy,
We just praise the Lord for the way he led in planning and leading in last week's retreat!

We were happy before, but now we have a deeper appre-
ciation and understanding of each other. We have been
helped in understanding each other's personality. We're not
only enjoying each other's love more, but it has also helped
us to understand God's love more. Speaking for myself, I
have never felt so free! It's great to know David understands
me, and greater yet to know God loves me!

That group visited together until about 3:15 p.m. Sunday
afternoon. During this time it was suggested that we meet in
a few weeks to encourage each other. All the families are
coming to our house for a potluck supper.

We also agreed that we'd like another retreat in three to
five years with the exact group. We'd like you to keep this in
mind and remember each of us in prayer as you think of us!

Thank you for all your quiet, gentle love and understanding. Thanks for helping us to understand ourselves and each
other. We'll never be the same!

It's been our pleasure to learn to know you. We pray
God's blessing upon you as you continue to help others!

Love,
David and Iva

Often marriages must be renewed, or reborn, not
repaired. Yes, in the day-to-day experience many repairs are
needed. "I'm sorry, did I hurt you?" "I didn't know being
late would cause this much chaos!" Or simply, "How do you
feel today?" However, that is not always sufficient.

At least once in a marriage the ultimate issue of what two
people need in life in relation to each other has to be
confronted. Then a great leap of faith must be made that finally reaches to the very depth of their beings. "Above all
else on earth, I love you. We are made for each other from
time eternal to time eternal. It was meant that you and I
travel this little earthly space together—for our good, for the
good of our children that follow us, and for the universal
plan of all mankind and all existence—so help us, God!"

How deep the valley is that needs to be crossed depends on each couple—the unique personality of each individual and the way they interact with each other. For some it may be relatively shallow and yet the deepest agenda will have been met. We meet those for whom the valleys are deep and the journey excruciatingly painful. We have traveled through this valley with many couples and then stood on the mountain peak, stretching our eyes from the horizon of the past to the horizon of the future, and marveled at the beautiful sight.

When does one hit bottom? That too is unique for each couple; but it is not hard to locate. On a marriage retreat weekend it is not unusual for couples to predict where they are heading and how deep the valley is that lies before them.

The main thing that we wish to communicate is now that we know the meaning of the journey—the necessity of the valley of suffering and the reward of the mount of transfiguration—let us take the leap of faith that is necessary for our particular marriage.

For reflection and discussion

The term *rebirth* is often used to describe conversion to following Christ. What human and divine realities are associated with rebirth in this sense (for example, repentance, forgiveness, grace)? How might these apply to the rebirth of a marriage? How were they present in Dave and Iva's story? How might they be applied in your family so that a relationship may be reborn?

11

When the Nest Empties

Because it need not be traumatic when children leave, we have not called this chapter "The Empty Nest Syndrome." Actually, as children and parents take the next step in a healthy growth experience, all can benefit.

It is possible to look at the reaction to leaving as a continuum. At the one extreme is the healthy way of staying and at the other extreme is the unhealthy way of leaving. There are a number of variations between these extremes.

Healthy staying. It has been established that adolescence is ending later and later. At the turn of the century adolescence ended at sixteen. It is now assumed to end at twenty-five. As a result, parents have to be ready to have their children stay home longer. It may require Christian compassion, sensitive dialogue, and perhaps much personal sacrifice to make this possible.

We are also in an era when the choice for staying single is becoming a more acceptable norm. If our children choose that path, should not the household remain open to them to live this lifestyle? The books on creative singleness are warning us of another forthcoming social change. More persons will choose not to marry at all.

Far too many marriages are functioning poorly because the couple never thought that singleness was an option for them. It is not uncommon to see a couple in marriage counseling where the husband is a confirmed bachelor in his heart. For some unknown reason he now happens to have a wife. With a little exploring it becomes evident that he followed the unwritten code that he had to date, propose after a certain length of time, and then marry. Suddenly he wakes up to the fact that he does not want to be married.

Painful staying. To stay home when it is wrong for the child, the parents, or both, can be very painful. It is not unusual for a child to transform the recreation room into a bachelor pad and then live a lifestyle that is completely out of keeping with all of the values that are believed and practiced one floor above. One such scene of which we became aware is symbolized by loud gospel music being played on the first floor to drown out the rock music on the floor below. In the recreation room the opposite occurs. The contest gets worse as each increases the volume to declare their territorial rights and also as a way of communicating their values to each other.

Unhealthy staying. One of the most unhealthy situations is when the parents have built into their beings the need to keep children at home. Instead of the child having the strength to flee, he or she surrenders and acquiesces to complete dependency. Then after a decade the child is so dependent that he or she can never leave. Therefore, the nest is never empty as long as the parents live. Adult single persons may find themselves wondering what it would have been like had they asserted themselves several decades earlier.

Healthy leaving. Healthy leaving is best illustrated by children who leave home in a manner and at a time that are right for everyone. Children need to be emotionally mature enough to leave and ready to choose a manner of leaving that is not harmful to themselves or their parents.

For example, the oldest daughter of a local family met the son of a very similar family at a Christian high school. From the moment that the courtship began there was a sigh of relief and many words of approval came from both households. Neither family could have asked for more. Since both children had always been compliant by nature, they gained a lot of satisfaction from receiving such heartfelt approval. Courtship centered on seeing each other as much as possible at school, participating in school social functions, and also becoming very active in church youth activities. In keeping with the aspirations of both families, each accepted employment immediately upon graduation. His job had adequate possibilities for advancement to the level his father had achieved. Both continued living at home for three and a half years as they saved money and planned for the day when they would be married. The wedding day was a time when two large family groups came together to celebrate a new bond between them. This also was the occasion for two young adults nearing their twenty-second birthdays to leave the nest and establish their own home not far from each of their families of origin.

When the oldest of several children leaves, it is easier because there is no empty nest which results. It is not uncommon for parents to breathe a sigh of relief, because they are ready for less household commotion.

Painful leaving. The fourth son of some friends illustrates a very different leaving process. The oldest three boys adopted the family norms fairly well. They entered college, as both parents had a generation earlier. They selected majors that were in keeping with the extreme achievement orientation of both parents. Then they slowly worked their way to the outside.

The last son had always exhibited an acute individuality. He always did things his way and that was usually very different. So the parents had time to anticipate that his leaving also had to be unique.

When this son chose not to enroll in college, and purchased a van instead, his exit method became clear. The diligence with which he refurbished the van was his way of telling his parents that he was leaving. To talk things through with them also had never been his style. So why should he do that now? When a buddy joined in the project, it became apparent that they were exiting together.

True to form, only weeks after graduation, the parents were informed that traveling west was his style of leaving. It took careful negotiating by the parents to gain a promise that he would call home collect once every three months to tell them where they were living and what they were doing to survive, provided the parents promised not to pry.

When he left, the house was empty for the first time, and the parents felt it keenly. Fortunately they had spent years evolving very productive lives, so they had interesting diversions awaiting.

Currently, one of the more common events is that children leave home repeatedly because they do not make it on their own and must return home again. This may be painful. However, due to the difficult socioeconomic conditions today, it is a pattern that must be anticipated. The process actually can be guided so that it becomes healthy for everyone.

Our second daughter chose this route. She left for a

college about 300 miles away. Unlike the oldest daughter, she kept a multitude of ties in the home community and kept the college crowd more at arm's length. She returned home frequently and kept all her social ties in good repair. After four years, she moved in to stay, in the room which she had decorated to her own very special taste. This room always belonged to her far more than any room belonged to any of our other children.

Our stance was to welcome her home and assure her that her spot in the home was hers indefinitely. Now, four years later, she is making wedding plans and preparing to move to a very unique home. The gift to us was that she delayed for two years our having to deal with the empty nest.

There are many families that have to deal with returning children. It takes a lot of sensitivity to cope with children who have come back acutely bruised by the outside world. When it is a painful leaving process, it often requires the true love of Christ to enter the household in a very special way to enable the outcome to be redemptive. For example, it took a great deal of God's love and grace for a forty-four-year-old couple to adopt the newborn infant of a daughter who brought it home after she fled the family home against her parents' wishes. She needed to be free of this toddler to begin again. Now she is beginning responsibly and with professional help.

Unhealthy leaving. There are many families who create unhealthy climates for children to leave. In these families the leaving becomes as unhealthy as the environment of the years that preceded.

One of the most destructive statements a parent can make to a child is, "If you don't want to do as I tell you, then get out of here." However, our experience shows that this is a rather common event. Often a marriage itself is already so exhausting to parents that the normal acting out of an older adolescent child is just too much. When this happens, the straw breaks.

Yet there are times when a family is so fragile that a child must be asked to leave. At the very worst extreme is the situation when a child is bringing drugs into the household and is addicted. The child who cannot or will not seek treatment may not only have to be asked to leave; he or she may have to be firmly but kindly told not to return until the child can show evidence of complete recovery.

On the other side, parents can also create a family lifestyle that makes healthy leaving impossible. There are many persons who build the need for their children into their own personalities to such an extent that the children know they cannot leave and have one or both parents survive. Since the drive for independent survival takes precedence over surrender to parents' needs, these children may suddenly bolt from the household in a very impulsive, unrealistic way.

What about the empty nest syndrome? Is it an inevitable event that all families must prepare to face? Most likely the nest will empty, but this need not be unhealthy. What happens should surely not be called a syndrome.

What we envision is that parents will want to prepare themselves in such a way that their lives with each other will become enriched and life in the outside world will enlarge as the number of persons in the household diminishes. This is also healthy for children to watch. They need to get the clear message that they can leave without guilt because nothing is collapsing behind them. I believe our children get the distinct message that we roll out the carpet for them as they return from college. But they also see us poised to roll it back up again an hour after they leave.

We believe that one good test of parents' psychological readiness is the attitude they take toward a child's bedroom as they are entering their twenties. The over-possessive parent who is prone to have an empty-nest reaction will very carefully keep the bedrooms completely intact, just like they were when the children left. If children leave for a brief or long period, they come home to find that the room has been very tenderly restored to its original condition. The unconscious message the children get is, "We need you in that bedroom, preferably not grown up." The clincher is when a mother places the favorite doll, that never got thrown away, on the bed while the child is away.

A healthy view is to begin surmising out loud how that bedroom can double as a guest room or perhaps a television hideaway or den. The other extreme is to quickly begin measuring the room for a home office when the child may be talking about a trial experience away from home.

Years before children grow up, parents need to preview the future and prepare to live without them. If parents have lost the art of dialogue, it needs to be learned. Parents can very easily adopt their children as communication links between each other. The wife may say, "One of these days I'm going to have to teach your father manners that are appropriate for you children to copy," while her husband is at the opposite end of the table. Then when the children are gone, parents have to face each other for the first time in many years. They may find that they don't know how to talk to each other.

The empty nest may not be filled with children, but it does not have to stay empty. Two people in their late forties or fifties must find a way of filling it with each other and all of the other filling material available to them. This takes foresight, caring, ingenuity, and creativity.

For reflection and discussion

If you still have your summary from chapter 1, go back to it and review the "emptying the nest" experiences. How was the leaving processed? What were the long-term effects? If persons are preparing to "leave the nest" now, how are you responding (even if you are the person leaving)? What ties are being severed? What bridges are being built?

12

Creative Closure

A pastor friend had a sudden awakening about the potential of old age. As he was walking down the street after a six-inch snowfall, he came upon an elderly lady who was shoveling her sidewalks while supporting herself with a walker. She could only take a small amount with each attempt and could only go a very short distance before she needed to move her walker ahead. Every move was carefully calculated and perfectly executed. The pastor was overwhelmed with compassion and offered to do the shoveling for her.

The lady turned toward him, her face radiating with zeal, enthusiasm, and excitement, as she exclaimed, "Pastor, I've been waiting for the snow to fall for weeks so that I could shovel my walks. You see, I have shoveled it several times since it started to snow. I wouldn't miss this for anything!"

The pastor groped for a response and finally said, "Isn't old age awful?"

She responded, "That's up to each person to decide. This is the best life I have ever lived. I spent my whole life rushing from one obligation to the next. Now I have no obligations. I do everything because I want to do it. This snow is my challenge now, and I love it. Before, I didn't know what life was all about. Now I live every moment to the fullest. Every shovelful is a delight. Every snowflake is beautiful to look at. I cherish every moment I am alive because there are only a few left. I now notice the smallest things, which I never saw before. I'm touched by every word people say, by every smile, and by you being so concerned about me. I am more alive now than ever."

The pastor then caught on to what was happening and said, "You know, this is strange. I was going to help you and it turned out that I was the one in need of help. You helped me. I needed you to tell me what really matters in life. May I use this event in my sermon on Sunday? You preached a powerful message to me."

The woman's response was perfectly consistent: "Do as you like, pastor, to live your life; but allow me to shovel my walk."

The message of this woman is that the aging process has a strong contradiction built into it. The body does, in fact, deteriorate; but the soul of a person does not have to go with the body. It can be renewed over and over again. The choice, as this woman said, belongs to each person.

Western culture does not know this truth. Here, the value of life is tied to age—what the body looks like and what one can do. So aging is too frequently viewed solely as a deteriorating process. Other cultures tune in on the aliveness of the soul as a measure of the true worth of a person. The aging process is revered because the person is growing in wisdom, maturity, and value. Older persons can see truth from a lofty vantage point that the young do not have.

In our culture, where accumulation of information takes precedence over wisdom, the young replace the old in an ever more rapid pace. Collecting, storing, and retrieving in-

formation and manipulating systems are revered. In this setting aging is a liability and youth has much greater value.
The aging process must be disguised, avoided, or denied
rather than valued.

However, like every other stage in family life, it is those
who have lived each of the earlier stages to the full who are
ready for the next stage. Those persons who have lived a full
life can come to the last stage and bring it to an appropriate
closure. Persons whose individual and family lives are empty
dread the thought that all must come to an end. How can
you end family life if you have never really lived it? A good
model is to look at life as an ever renewing possibility and to
use each event for a new beginning.

You can choose to feel good that life can be brought to a
closure. This means to bring every area to an appropriate
ending. Many people do not do this. Instead, they grieve
over every item that must be left behind. The healthier attitude is to look at every ending and be thankful for the
freedom to move on. So when you realize that you cannot
make the large family dinners any longer because your
children say it's their turn, you simply say, "Thank you,
Lord, that I do not have to do that anymore. I once loved
doing it, and I have fond memories; but it's their turn now."
At retirement, you reflect, "I do not need to go to work anymore. It may snow or sleet, or the wind may howl, and I can
stay where it's warm. Let the young people take over at the
plant. Let them struggle with the multitude of problems.
They will get their rewards; but it is not for me any longer.
Thank you, Lord, for peace of soul!"

No one can ever accomplish all that she or he had planned
or all that is possible to have done in a lifetime. We have
only to do our part and leave the rest to others. The future
belongs to the next generation. We may not understand

them or their world, but that too is all right.

To be resigned to one's stage in life does not mean giving up or going into despair. This world was never meant to be a permanent residence for anyone. Here we have a promising beginning, a productive middle, and then a diminishing ending stage.

However, every ending is a new beginning. Every person can choose to meditate on the ending or contemplate the new beginning. The elderly lady with the walker chose to live in the new life when she no longer needed to rush around and capture the world and now had the privilege to appreciate the smallest things. She suddenly found joy in something that once was only a nuisance.

New beginnings in the later stages of life may mean different things. For some it may mean doing what they never had time to do but always wanted to. We just heard about an elderly couple who sold their home and are taking their boat down the inland waterways to one of the Southern states. They plan to spend a year living on the boat as they explore the rivers and lakes until they find a place to settle. Most persons won't have the desire or the means to do this, but it illustrates that there are certain privileges that come with retirement.

For others, a new beginning may be an opportunity to marry again after losing a lifelong mate. This may be a good idea if they first discover whether they are good companions. In early marriages, a large variety of motives are involved. In a marriage in later life, companionship should be the central motive. This means that two persons simply examine what they like to do in life. Two persons should ask themselves, "What do we want to do with the remainder of our lives?" If the answers generally are alike, then remarriage to each other may be right. If one yearns to travel around the world

and the other is a homebody, such a match is heading for
trouble. For young persons, "Because we love each other" is
a poor excuse to marry. Later in life, it is an even poorer
reason. "Because our lives match" is far better.

Death represents the end of family life. Though you may
have no choice as to when or how this may occur, you can do
a lot ahead of time that will affect the family when death
comes. Just permitting yourself to reflect on the inevitability
of death is already a way of beginning to deal with it. To talk
about death within the family is an even more effective
preparation.

One of the best ways to prepare for death within the
family is to have a family gathering at the time that the
family will is rewritten. At such a time the stage is perfectly
set to have dialogue with all family members. Then the
exact wishes of everyone can be sorted out in preparation for
the inevitable. Parents then need to spell out how they view
their possessions and their obligations to each family
member. One key factor that must be faced is the value that
they place on the work of the church and their intention to
make a contribution to it. The overall message that is communicated in such dialogue is that death is coming and it is
the parents' hope that everyone who remains will continue
to live by the values that were lived throughout each of the
earlier stages of family life.

There are many destructive traditions in families that
come from earlier practices. One of these was the parents'
keeping the contents of a will secret and their children hos-
tage to it. One son gave his life working for his dad on the
large family farm that was worth a fortune, under the
assumption that it would eventually be his. He had forfeited
many choices because he assumed that this was his price to

pay to get what he thought was coming to him. Although he never was certain whether that was his dad's intention, he continued working. He thought he knew his dad. The other family members chose to find their places in the world. When the will was finally read, the farm was divided equally with no regard to the son who had exchanged his life for an assumed promise. There are many sad accounts of families that were torn apart by events like this and never again re-united.

It just may be helpful to write out in full how you would like death to come if you had complete choice. The very act of writing this is a very healthy experience because it forces you to contemplate every aspect of death. To share it with family members adds another dimension.

Al had been preparing for this final drama for many years. Early in life he made a commitment to Jesus Christ as his Savior and Lord. Then in his own simple way he lived out his commitment as a farmer and laborer. This fact was clear to his wife and three daughters throughout his life.

In his mid-fifties, this father began experiencing heart failure. There were clear warning signals that there was a real possibility of a sudden end. During that time a peaceful glow appeared to come over him. The neighbors who were used to seeing him ride his lawn mower now noticed that his singing of gospel songs was louder and more exuberant. The thought often crossed their minds that this man was really riding his mower to glory.

At fifty-eight he had to be hospitalized for acute chest pains. Soon after this, he suffered a severe heart attack. The "Code 9" life team responded as they were trained and re-vived him. Somewhere in the midst of this, he exclaimed, "It's beautiful. I'm going home. Hallelujah! It's beautiful!"

When he was revived, Al's words were filled with sadness, at first. "Oh," he moaned, "I'm coming back. Do I have to come back?" Then he addressed the attending physician, "Doctor, why did you do that?"

"Do what?" the physician asked.

"Did you have to bring me back?" Al then reached for the physician's hand and asked him, "Doctor, do you love Jesus?"

The physician answered, "Yes, Al, I do."

He then turned to the nurses around his bed and asked them the same question. After he got a positive answer, he exclaimed. "Oh, isn't it wonderful to be cared for by a doctor and nurses who all love Jesus." After that Al described his experience which has now become known as "a life-after-life experience."

Al felt himself departing his hospital bed at the moment that the attack occurred. He traveled upward on a long passageway, which ended in a large bright space. According to Al, this was heaven. He knew beyond a doubt that he was in the promised land. A sensation told him that Jesus was present even though he could not specifically see or identify him. There were many people who were rejoicing because they were there and also because he had arrived. They were expressing their joy with the same gospel songs he used to sing at church and while riding the mower. He also had a distinct impression that God was also present, but some distance away and probably in a more sacred place.

Suddenly he got the sensation that it was not time yet for him to remain there and that he had to leave and return to earth. There was something he had to do before he could stay. So he felt himself departing and he awoke in his hospital bed. He now told the story of the beautiful venture he had experienced to everyone who would listen.

After that he cried much of the time. The nurses were not sure why. Probably it was due to his very deep ambivalent emotions. It must have been too great a contrast to experience the full peace and glory of heaven and then the pain of life with a failing body.

Several more heart attacks followed, and each time he was revived. Each time he awoke to tell of another journey to the promised land. When he was not fully aware of his surroundings, he took the hand of one of the nurses and addressed her as if she were his wife. "Darling, I should have a tape recording. People will never believe this experience; but if I had it on tape they might."

From his bedside there radiated shock waves that deeply affected a multitude of people. The persons who stood around the bed called it marvelous. The family was overwhelmed, not knowing whether to rejoice or mourn. His pastor and congregation were revitalized with a new sense of Jesus' presence and the Holy Spirit's power. The larger community was eagerly picking up bits and pieces and passing them on—in total disbelief, with uncertainty, or rejoicing to have caught a glimpse of eternity.

The family, including Al, concluded that it was God's will that another resuscitation should not be done following the next heart stoppage. His heart was damaged so badly that he could never be normal again. One doctor suggested a pacemaker, but he could not even give them the assurance that Al would live until he got to the operating room. To this final suggestion, Al responded, "Absolutely not!" with the full assurance that this was God's will as he and his wife knew it.

The family now surrendered peacefully to "thy will be done," which meant to let Al go where he so much longed to go. This world was no longer for him. He had already caught a glimpse of the place prepared for him; and it was beautiful, peaceful, and restful. With all the suffocating chest pains, he so much welcomed relief.

As the family was going through one of the most difficult lessons of spiritual surrender, the pastor led Al's spiritual family, the congregation, in a ritual of yielding. At the beginning of the church service, the pastor told them: "Many of you have been continuing in concern for Al. He has had several further attacks yesterday and again late last night. He is very weak and low. This morning a member of the family called and their request is that we have special prayer for his comfort and peace. They pray that he will be able to meet the Lord in that peace that he has found and has experienced in very deep ways over the last while. So with this family's request and desire in mind, we will take a moment now, on behalf of Al and his family.

"Our God, we thank you this morning for the intercession of Jesus, our Lord, at your right hand and the communication of your Holy Spirit, who knows your mind and will. We lay before you in trust our brother Al and ask that according to his family's and his desire you will grant to him your peace and rest. We pray, Lord, that he may receive the confidence of the arms of Jesus upholding him, the rest of his Lord sustaining him, and that the hope that you have promised to all who trust in you might be his in a deep and abiding way this hour. We commend him into your care and keeping, thanking you, even as your apostle Paul has said, that whether by life or death you have created us to glorify your name and to bring praise for your mercies and goodnesses in our lives. Grant him relief from pain and suffering.

"We pray for his wife and family. Grant to each one that peace that passes all understanding and keeps and guards and overrules our hearts and minds in Christ Jesus, to whom we give praise and thanksgiving. In his Name. Amen."

At the moment that Al was breathing his last several painful breaths, a member of his congregation experienced an
unmistakable call to prayer. "I was driven to my knees and it
was clear to me that I was to ask for his release. And so I
did." And so Al died.

This illustration shows how a profound transformation occurred on the deathbed of one Christian. The effect of this
then spread to his wife, their children, and the other family
members. It even spread to the hospital staff, his congregation, and to the larger community.

The intent is not to arouse debate around life-after-life
phenomena, but to show that Al prepared for his death. He
did this openly and engaged his family in the process. Then
when the end came, the whole family was ready to enter
into it with the openness that had always been present. Profound family renewal is possible even during the last moments of life.

For reflection and discussion

The task of the Christian throughout life is to use faithfully
whatever resources he or she has at a particular point. One task of
a Christian family is to assist each other in faithful living
throughout the life cycle. These tasks are positive, not negative,
because they involve helping each other recognize and accept
God's grace. Evaluate the summary you prepared for chapter 1
from this perspective.

13

The Challenge

The challenge in family living is to view the family as ever evolving and to always look for new opportunities for growth. The healthy view is to see the family as a fluid, flexible unit whose shape is always changing. This leaves the system ready to respond to any individual's special need or to the needs of the entire family unit. Then there is no danger of anyone digging into a hopeless rut.

With this type of model for family life, how can you ever be certain that you have done the right thing? Or how can you rest with the assurance that all will be well with your family in the future?

In one sense, no family may ever have this luxury. Life is simply too complex for all family members to have this type of certainty. Although we have been educated in family living, have helped many persons in therapy, have conducted workshops, and have endeavored to live this model with diligence, we have no assurance that we may not have to deal with a divorce in our own family. So, in the absolute sense, one never has a guarantee of the future.

Yet in another sense persons can have the assurance that

they have prepared their family to live with change regardless of what that might be. The family who learns to live with change, then becomes aware that crises do not cause the collapse of persons or the disintegration of the family unit. The inner strength of the family gives family members the assurance that somehow they will rise above whatever may face them. Then the tragedy itself, no matter how great, also has the potential to bring forth fruit.

Dark clouds will pass over every family. The question is only how the family will respond. Will difficulty lead to crippling paralysis or to a search for the silver lining?

Now we want to close with the story of how one family adapted when a drastic change became mandatory. They had no promise that they would find the silver lining, but they chose to surrender all the comforts of a lifestyle that they had spent years building. In one dramatic event they risked it all with no promise for the future.

The story of Lawrence and Clarice is an appropriate one to conclude this study of family renewal. Their actual names have been used because it would be impossible to hide their identities. Many persons have observed their drama as it unfolded. We are grateful for their permission to use the story and for their assistance in maintaining accuracy.

Lawrence and Clarice spent more than twenty busy years in Pennsylvania in farming and in business with their family of seven children. They acquired their farm from Lawrence's side of the family, so it held many precious memories. He grew up there, and acquired his farming and handyman skills there. His father relinquished the farming operation to him, and the parents built their retirement home on adjoining land. This was symbolic of family closeness spanning three generations.

They acquired a laundry and dry-cleaning business as a place to direct the energies of Clarice and the children as they reached their teens. This model of family life fitted the community norms, so why should they consider a change?

There was other activity in this home. The family farm also became home for foster children. The attachment that developed between this family and the "borrowed" children was so intense that one mother of a placed child turned to them for her own care and nurture. Not only did her children need a home like this, she did also.

In addition to the three children born to them, they had acquired four more by adoption. Even as they were struggling with the implications of making an enormous transition, another child became available for adoption. As might be anticipated, they proceeded with the adoption although the future of the entire family was uncertain.

Gradually a new calling began to surface. Lawrence emerged as a leader in their home congregation. On committees, he often guided the process to resolution and was elected to be chairperson. He also taught an adult class. Clarice invested many precious moments of her busy schedule with persons in need. It might be one of her children struggling with a crisis, or persons in the congregation or community who sought her when the burden was too big to bear alone.

Through intense dialogue in a small group, a distinct calling began to emerge for Lawrence and Clarice. They were called to sell all they had, both farm and business, to leave the state for advanced seminary training. This meant total disruption of the lives of seven children, including everything they had ever known, to begin again. The possibility for full-time ministry in the future was uncertain. Not one congregation in their home area had suggested a possible opening. Nevertheless, they heard the call loud and clear from a higher source. With no light on the horizon, they moved ahead. The following statement appeared in the seminary bulletin.

> The decision to come to seminary was a momentous one for Lawrence and Clarice. In addition to the normal pains of uprooting, it meant facing the possibility of a major shift in vocational focus from something in which they had proven their abilities to a ministry of unknown shape. It also meant facing the demands of graduate level courses with a high-school education. The transition to seminary studies involved anxiety and pain. The change from activities in which they had expertise to pursuits in which they had little experience has been a major challenge. They struggled with new ideas and vocabulary and the need to develop a range of new study and organizational skills. They found the professors responsive to their needs and an acceptance in the seminary community which was not limited by their modest educational experience.
>
> Clarice has found the struggle exhilarating as well as painful as she feels the call and the resources to move beyond familiar role expectations and experiences—the vitality of a new beginning. Lawrence too has experienced the invigorating effect of personal growth as he works at answers to questions about ministry. They sense the preparation may be leading them into ministry with church planting and the emerging church.

After completion of seminary, they accepted a call to a shared pastorate in a congregation in an urban setting 800 miles from their home community. The preaching assignment is also on an alternate week basis.

There is no question that this monumental change of direction for such a large family at mid-life carries extreme stress, risk, and uncertainty. At times they saw only the

ominous cloud, but there was a silver lining. Their reward
was not in this world's goods. Let them speak for themselves—first Lawrence.

> Our two years of seminary have stretched and prodded us to
> deeper levels of commitment to God, to each other, to our
> family, and to the church. We are grateful for this op-
> portunity to change careers and accept our call to pastoral
> ministry. So along with our celebration of twenty-five years
> of marriage, we are also celebrating our graduation from
> seminary and a new beginning of life together as we serve
> our risen Jesus together in shared pastoral ministry. The
> most important thing for us is the joy of continuing to work
> together with the one we love. In ministry and in marriage
> two signs of God's grace stand side by side in Christian com-
> munity.
>
> In crises, despair wants to come through, but we are
> learning to identify it and go past it to a sense of hope. We
> think it comes from learning to trust our inner wisdom—a
> wisdom that is just beginning to emerge.

Clarice adds another dimension.

> Working through life with my children has given me a
> greater sense of who I am. It has helped me work at my
> identity, while helping them discover theirs or freeing them
> to do so. To have my adult son tell me he wants to learn to
> know me as a person, and not just Mom, is gratifying to me.
> To relate to my children as peer is a new and positive
> experience. I think the thing that sent me into areas that
> were untouchable for my family was my responsibility as a
> mother. I wanted more than anything to have a happy
> satisfying experience for everyone. Not one without conflict,
> but one that faces it head-on and deals with it in a positive
> way—a family that feels together, cares together, cries to-
> gether, laughs together, plays together, and works together.
> This is something we work at together as a caring com-
> munity of people.

I work hard at changing traditional roles. Family for me has become a context for salvation: a significant arena in which God's life-giving, renewing, and healing work goes on. I face this time of my life with a sense of hope.

There has been a penalty to pay for all this. Most of the time I have learned to face criticism with an inner peace, because I think I'm developing a sense of hope that it will turn out for the best. It has been a lonely path to take, but I have discovered I can have a family of caring brothers and sisters and parents within Christian community, and this has been far greater than anything I could have anticipated.

As I am in this mid-life time of life, it is again a new era. Lawrence and I have taken a serious look at the direction we were going and at the rat race we were caught in. Then we realized that there has to be more to life than this for us. Things weren't adding up. There was too much life yet to be lived. We chose to make some radical changes. It required a lot of self-discipline and patience.

To be the person God intended me to be is what I am striving for. To develop my uniqueness as a woman and to help others begin that process is an awesome responsibility—one I can help to bring about. Life is constantly growing, developing, and changing.

I've learned that most growth comes in the midst of facing the pain.

For reflection and discussion

What is the major challenge facing your family now? How have you responded to this point? What have been the effects? What changes might you consider since you have completed this study?

The Authors

Family life has always been a crucial concern for Abraham and Dorothy Schmitt. They were deeply involved in their families of origin, as well as the entire kinship system. They are also committed to their chosen family.

For Abraham, the extended family included one third of the village of Blumenort, Saskatchewan, Canada. There was no mystery about where he belonged. Grandparents were across the road; aunts and uncles, first and second cousins were up and down the road. The more distant relatives were known to all as they spread to the neighboring villages of Blumenhof, Schoenfeld, and Rheinland. He knew his identity in terms of the entire family system.

It was not that much different for Dorothy who grew up in an early Mennonite settlement, the Franconia Conference, north of Philadelphia, Pennsylvania. Because of the stability of these people, she too was familiar with her roots. Later, the genealogical study of this family became a major family event as she guided the children in preparing a family tree dated to the original settlement in this area.

After graduating from Goshen College and Goshen

College Biblical Seminary, Abraham completed his master's and doctoral studies at the University of Pennsylvania. Continuing his interest in family life, he took specialized training in marriage counseling and family therapy. This led to a professorship at that same school which included a heavy teaching assignment in the specialty of personality development and family dynamics. The next step was to open his own office to practice in this field, now a full-time assignment. The birth of four children immersed both of them in firsthand experience in family life. Now the nest is almost empty.

Writing articles and books has become important to both Abraham and Dorothy at their present stage in life. A joint statement, "This Kept Us Married" was published in *The Christian Reader.*

With Dorothy's organizational, editing, and typing skills, Abe has published *Dialogue with Death, The Art of Listening with Love,* and *Before I Wake.* Jointly they have written *When a Congregation Cares: A new approach to crisis ministries* (Herald Press, 1984).

One of the most unusual early experiences involving writing was the release of an article "Conflict and Ecstasy: A Model for a Maturing Marriage." This was printed and reprinted in five different Christian magazines. Since then more than 8,000 reprints of this article have been requested and distributed.

They made their first major impact on the wider church by conducting weekend marriage enrichment workshops in eastern U.S.A. This led to an invitation to write a chapter, "Marriage Renewal Retreats," in Herbert Otto's book, *Marriage and Family Enrichment: New Perspectives and Programs* (1976, Abingdon). They have jointly led many other growth groups.